Impossible to Swallow
Collection of Short Stories about
the White Terror in Taiwan

C. J. Anderson-Wu

In Memory of My Parents

Preface

I hope I don't have to write more about white terror, yet....

White terror in Taiwan, the terrible oppression of freedom of speech, was followed by the 228 clash in 1947. The number of deaths during the conflicts and in the martial law period (1949~1987) afterward is still unclear.

This collection of short stories is about how it impacted the lives of ordinary people.

8
Judge Not

26
Blue Eyes

45
First Lady

60
Wednesdays

76
Those Healed and Unhealed

97
Impossible to Swallow

131
Legacy

151
Others' Guilt

169
A Letter From Father

174
About the Author

Judge Not

On that Tuesday morning, he took newspapers from the mailbox and read through them while having breakfast. On the front page the headline was "Instigators of Sedition Indicted", next to it was international news, "Soviet Union Rejects Withdraw of Troops from Afghanistan, Jimmy Carter Warns That US Might Boycott Moscow Olympic Games". Exactly one year ago, Jimmy Carter decided to build a formal relation with the Chinese Communist regime. This person had betrayed Taiwan, he thought, and now he thinks to contain the evil of Communism?

The complete indictment was printed on the third page, very short, saying the editor-in-chief of the *Formosa Magazine* had been running an eel farming business in Japan to cover up their collusion with the communists from China. It explained how the eight indicted were connected to one another through various underground organizations in Japan or in the US under the disguise of the business of the magazine. The magazine had been banned as its purpose was the overthrow of the government and seizure of power, but they continued spreading seditious words. In later paragraphs it said all the eight people, six men and two women, had short-term, mid-term and long-term plans to disturb people's trust in the government by causing conflicts in the society in order to achieve their goal of Taiwan's independence.

So were they communists or separatists? A sense of contempt rose inside him. Could prosecutors nowadays perhaps try to be more logical and conscientious? If these people were working with communists from China, they couldn't be working for the independence of Taiwan because Chinese Communism was determined to take over Taiwan, even bloodshed was necessary. Didn't they see the paradox? An indictment for eight people, that was all they could do? He also felt disgusted by those indicted. What did they really want? Why would they plant poisonous seeds in our society? Why would they be so naive as to collude with communists? What made them think Taiwan was not a part of China? Blasphemy! Blasphemous criminals and stupid prosecutors.

Hearing the bus outside, he put down the newspapers and grabbed his briefcase, running outside to catch the bus. It was the bus transporting himself along with his neighbors, all of whom were his colleagues in legal practice, to the courts from the government subsidized housing blocks in which they lived. They were mostly judges, he himself was one of the chief judges of the fifteen courts of criminal appeals. He wondered if his fellow judges would talk about the lousy indictment in today's newspapers, but this morning they were quiet. He gathered that they hadn't read it yet.

From the bus window he saw Chien Hsin-Hwan take off with his motorcycle, it was later than the time he usually took off. It was a cold morning although it was almost the end of winter. Chien was his next door neighbor, occupying a smaller family unit than his own because Chien was younger and still was a district attorney. At 46, Chien was not young as most district attorneys, most of his peers had already got promoted to the Department of Justice in the central government or became judges of district courts, but Chien's position hadn't changed for a long time. It was probably because Chien spent too much time reading books unrelated to the profession, he thought. In addition to those philosophical publications, Chien also read a lot of books that he asked his friends to buy and mail to him from Japan. When the Japanese retreated from Taiwan Chien was almost a teenager, he had been educated in Japanese. He continued studying Japanese by himself and was quite familiar with Japanese laws.

Chien's children as well as his own went to the same junior high school although he was already in his late fifties. That was because he spent eight years fighting against Japan and another several years running from the Chinese communist troops. By the time he settled in Taiwan he was in his late thirties. With wars, everything in life started late if it started at all.

It was unusually quiet in the office, even though the most argumentative judges were in his court. Usually their day began with discussions about the legal issues they saw from the morning newspapers. Perhaps they did not care about the indictment of the people from *Formosa Magazine* because their cases would be tried in courts-martial anyway? No, it was something else. There was uneasiness in the air.

His court was in recess today, he decided to use the time to find more information in the library about slander, defamation, libel and freedom of speech, if there were examples setting clear jurisprudential ideas about them. When he walked to the door, he turned to look at Huang Mei-Hsueh, the least senior judge in his court to see if she wanted to help him, but when his eyes set on her, she turned her head away, seeming not to want to be interrupted from what she was doing. He opened the door and walked out alone.

At the terrace outside of the library he saw a man walk passing by with a bunch of files under his arm, his profile looked familiar. The judge stopped, waiting for the man to walk near so he could recognize who he was and greet him. But once he stopped, the man took a sudden turn, and disappeared into the rooms at the other side.

On Thursday night he had an unexpected visitor, Consultant Chang. There were always such "consultants" showing up every now and then since he settled in Taiwan. At first he did not mind their asking around until one day his friend whose work sort of connected to the Secret Service ambiguously hinted to him that because he had lived in Hong Kong for two years before coming to Taiwan, the authorities were afraid he had been recruited by the Communist Party during that time, he was to be checked on until they made sure he was still loyal to his party. At first he thought his friend meant it took several months, at most a couple of years, but now it has been nearly three decades.

Consultant Chang politely entered his living room although not invited. He sat himself in front of the television that his wife was watching a cooking show demonstrating how to make Hunan food. They had to turn off the TV and his wife retreated to the kitchen after greeting the visitor. The judge never really talked about the missions of these consultants with his wife in case she'd worry.

Consultant Chang started the conversation with, "I am sent to see if Your Honor thinks there is improvement we can make for the courts and for the work of Your Honor." Chang liked to use the term to address him in the court, very absurd, but the judge did not want to correct him, he was not interested to hear any other more stupid titles this man could come up with.

"Oh, that. I think the library hasn't procured more updated publications for a long time." He replied instinctively knowing all-the-while that it was not really the concern of Consultant Chang. Chang was not there to interview him about what they could do to assist their increasingly burdening legal work. After a moment of silence, Consultant Chang spoke, "I am also here to ask your opinions about Attorney Chien."

"How about him?"

"He, he seems not very interested in getting promoted...."

Rather than replying, he waited to see what

Consultant Chang was up to.

"... we wonder..., I wonder if there is something else engages him?"

"I don't know about that."

"Never mind, never mind." Consultant Chang grinned. Then he asked about his children, how they were doing in schools, but not very sincerely, before he stood up to leave.

His wife came back to the living room to turn on the TV again, but the show was no longer teaching the cooking of Hunan dishes.

That night he dreamed of his older brother. They were playing in the river, competing over who could bear the coldness longer until their lips were frozen to purple, their bodies shaking. He was the youngest child in his family, and the brother closest to his age was two years older, they hung out together all the time. They played in the river a lot until the chill of winter forbade them. Once the trace of spring began to show, they adventured to the river again. They were lashed by their parents many times for risking their young lives, but it hardly stopped them.

He dreamed of his childhood and his brother often, and sometimes in his dreams his brother was drowned and washed away.

It had been thirty-one years. He never knew how his family in China was, and they never knew where he ended up. Are they still alive? Do they know I am still alive?

Not long ago one of his friends told him he mailed his letters to his relatives in the US and they mailed them to China. In this way he finally established contact with his family. The judge thought of doing the same thing, but he knew no one in the US and he did not know if he could trust his friend's relatives.

Awake in the night, he felt desperate. How come the government thought he could have been recruited by the Chinese communists? Didn't he lose his parents, his brothers and sisters because of the perils caused by communists?

The following weeks he couldn't help but pay more attention to Chien Hsin-Hwan. He did look odd sometimes. When they encountered each other in the neighborhood Chien seemed less friendly than usual. Chien was from a farming family in Tainan where his parents still worked in the fields. Each time they came to Taipei to visit him or he went home down south, he'd share some agricultural products his family grew with the judge's wife, who was from the rural county of northern Tainan. They exchange words in Taiwanese, a dialect the judge never could command.

He was once in a lecture Chien made about the controversies of the textbooks for grammar schools in Japan after the world war. Chien made a very clear analysis about the Japanese political climate over the past thirty years, such as how it blatantly engaged in censorship, despite the constitutional law prohibiting it. By broadening the definition of "obscenity" to include words about the past wrongdoings of the government so a wide range of publications were banned. The judge felt so sick that the Japanese government still denied the crimes it had committed during the war. It was its invasion that caused China to finally fall into the control of Communism, it was its invasion that forced him to leave his hometown without knowing when he would see his family again.

He admired Chien's Japanese language skills although it was the language of their former invading colonialists. It was important to know the judicial development in other societies. The judge did not know any foreign language well enough to do such research, he knew the only way for him to maintain competitiveness in his profession was to work harder.

The climate was getting warmer, and the time Chien left home for work seemed more irregular, but a district attorney needed to conduct investigations in person; the judge had been in the same position at one time. He also noticed that Chien had more visitors recently. Their community was a square-like structure of four stories with an atrium in the center, each story accommodated eight households. Chien's home was connected to his at their kitchen and back doors. One night when he took the trash out he noticed that once he got out, the TV of Chien's family was turned down. He did not give much thought to it, after all there were only three channels, what else could they watch? The trial of *Formosa Magazine* had lasted only nine days, but it was open to reporters under the pressure from the US, so he had been told.

Fifteen lawyers volunteered to defend the persecuted, and in addition to claiming that the defendants were tortured during their interrogations which was a serious violation of human rights, they questioned the justification of the Martial Law and the Courts-Martial, and contended that the trial should be moved to the High Court. The judge would like to take over the trial, he would look in-depth into how a person was guilty for being a separatist or a communist, compared to the lousy work of the prosecutors simply calling them "traitors" and "agitators" without explicating why and how they betrayed their country or agitated the public. How could a person to be led from his beliefs, no matter how absurd they were, to commit criminal activity? The defendant lawyers had been doing a great job, he thought, although he was clear in mind that the trial was not going to be moved to his court. He was appalled by the political standing of the eight defendants, especially their indirect denial that

Taiwan was culturally and historically related to China. Aren't we all the inheritors of Chinese legacy? Didn't we all benefit from the development and growth contributed by the Republic of China? Nonetheless, watching how the trial proceeded he also realized that the society should move forward and open up to different ideas.

But was it easy to open up to different ideas? At the beginning of school winter break, his daughter brought back a novel *Factory Men* by a Tainan writer. Her scores were not very good in the last semester, so he scolded her, "You should not read this crap. I am not like Attorney Chien who has family farmlands for his kids to inherit, if you don't study hard to acquire profession and earn your own living in the future, you are done."

"What is not crap to you anyway?" The high school girl had started her rebellious stage, "Is the work of any local writer just crap in your opinion?" He was not impressed by Taiwanese writers, he did not think their writing great enough to be among the classics, but works of contemporary Chinese writers were banned in Taiwan. He certainly was not a lover of Japanese literature, and works by western writers he once admired so much did not interest his children for they were so far away from their life experience.

Consultant Chang stopped by again a couple of weeks later. This time he made his point clear enough: to coax the judge to provide something against Chien Hsin-Hwan. "We have evidence that Chien has connection with these people hurting our country."

"What evidence?" asked the judge, and his question seemed to surprise Consultant Chang. Had he forgotten he was talking to a judge who demanded evidence invariably? The judge hardly revealed his contempt of the man sitting in front of him. Were they arresting more people?

Consultant Chang rummaged through his briefcase. It was a black leather case with the badge of the Nationalist Party. The suitcase was badly designed and roughly manufactured, just like all the gifts from the government. The wallet he was given for the anniversary of Taiwan Retrocession Day was a perfect example, an eyesore and very hard to use. Waste of good materials, he thought, looking at Consultant

Chang's black suitcase with regret.

Consultant Chang presented several pages of a paper on the desk. The judge read it through. It was about the formation of Japanese Constitution Law, under the supervision of General MacArthur after World War II. More than thirty years later now, there were people urging an amendment for more comprehensive coverage of human rights, such as the right to privacy (puraibashii-ken), the right to know or to access information (shirukenri), and lowering the legal age of adulthood from twenty to eighteen. Freedom of speech had been guaranteed as early as during the Meiji Reign, and was reemphasized in MacArthur's version of the constitution, which stated quite clearly: "all public officials shall be protected against unwarranted defamation." It was plausible research, and the judge knew that the only thing it could criminalize Chien for was its being published in the banned Autumn Issue of *Formosa Magazine* last year.

He was aware that Chien must be a sympathizer of the Formosa defendants, but by no means did an excellent paper, of which the paper in question was an example, prove his involvement in illegal activities.

"I don't see any connection in it, this is a high quality academic work," the judge returned the papers to Consultant Chang and added, not without sarcasm, "you must have seen the academic achievement in it as well."

Offended, Consultant Chang said in a threatening tone, "Covering up a felony is also a crime, allow me to remind you, Your Honor." Then he packed his briefcase and left.

The judge did not keep Consultant Chang's threat in mind at all. After all he had nothing to hide. The trial of *Formosa Magazine* took less than one month for the courts-martial to reach decisions, one of the defendants was sentenced to life, the rest of them were sentenced to twelve to fourteen years. It was said that their lives were spared because of the pressure from the US. All of them gave up the right to appeal. The judge did not think they deserved capital punishment, either, especially since the entire legal process went so badly; sub-quality, he would say. The author of the *Factory Men*, Yang Qinggchu, was also convicted at the criminal court as the accomplice of the seditionaries among another thirty-six people. His portraying of the workers as "the proletariat" became evidence of his connection with Communism. The judge was stunned, he wished his daughter had not kept that novel.

Chien Hsin-Hwan still acted oddly, if the judge's opinion was asked. He seemed to be more around their living quarters, but whenever they met, Chien always avoided eye contact with him. Was he a guilty man? What crimes could a person like him have committed? He was rather a dreamer than an action taker, a nerd than a conspirator. On the other hand, the judge knew that Consultant Chang would never stop hassling them, based on his own experience, despite the fact of the *Formosa Magazine* trial having ended. Several weeks passed and the judge and the attorney completely stopped interacting with one another, even their wives were aware of the growing strangeness between the two men and exchanged foods and cooking ideas much less.

In one early summer evening, when he was watering the plants in front of their back door, he saw a man with the same briefcase as Consultant Chang walk out of Chien's door. Immediately the judge realized that, given time, everyone in this island could have been found involved in certain schemes, that was how the nation operated. He felt cold sweat on his spine.

That night he dreamed of his brother and he swimming in the river again, only this time it was not his brother washed away, he himself was the one drowned.

First published by Eastlit Feb 2017

Blue Eyes

As she enters her mid-forties, her hair is starting to turn gray, and her vision depends more often on the aid of reading glasses. She feels herself fitting into Taiwan better now that her American look is fading, and her Taiwanese look is gradually taking over.

One morning on her way to work, she is standing at the subway platform when a woman about her age calls out to her, "Evelyn?" She stops with a gesture of affirmation, but she doesn't really recognize the woman.

"I am Yu-Jin, Cheng Yu-Jin. We went to the same elementary school."

"Oh, yeah. Cheng Yu-Jin. Why are you here? Do you often take this subway at this time? Why haven't we ever met before?" They quickly exchange information and realize that their offices are quite close to each other, so they decide they should have lunch together sometime.

Evelyn works for a literature publishing house. Her job is to read fiction written in English and write reports about each book she has read, expressing her opinion as to whether or not they should acquire the copyright and publish its Chinese version in Taiwan. In recent years, as the readership in China has quickly expanded, their copyright negotiations with foreign publishers often include the simplified Chinese version for readers in China. Sometimes they work with publishing houses in China, most of them state owned, and other times they compete against them for getting copyright authorization. Evelyn's judgement of marketable literary works is quite sharp. Usually the books she picks have satisfying sales, even those works that have been overlooked in the authors' own societies. That's probably because Evelyn made up stories, too. Evelyn wishes her company could publish more literary works with controversial issues, but the decision-makers don't want to take their chance in the market.

She gets a call from Cheng Yu-Jin less than a week later, so they meet in a restaurant that provides lunch with a free cup of coffee. Yu-Jin asks after Evelyn's mom.

"She is doing really well, totally independent and she knows how to have fun in life."

Evelyn's mother has just turned seventy, and she is still running a small general store back in their hometown, Tainan. Friends stop by to chat or to buy things, making the old-fashioned store a community hub as well as a gossip center. Actually, Evelyn doesn't think Cheng Yu-Jin ever met her mother; however, because of Evelyn's unusual look and her father's mysterious identity, she knows her mother must have been a topic of conversation in their school.

Yu-Jin pursues the subject further, "So you still have contact with your dad's family in the US?"

For a second Evelyn is speechless, but she recovers quickly enough, "Not much. The young generation hardly cares about families nowadays." At the same time she tries hard to recall which version of her story she had made up for Yu-Jin more than thirty-five years ago.

Yu-Jin looks straight at her eyes, saying in an excited tone, "My daughter is marrying a British man. I can't help thinking that, in a few years they might have babies with beautiful blue eyes similar to yours."

Evelyn feels dizzy. Yu-Jin thought her eyes were beautiful? She has no problem with the fact that her daughter is marrying a foreigner?

Evelyn's father was an American soldier who was stationed in the Tainan Air Force Base during the late 1960s to early 1970s, but she never wanted to admit that she was one of the illegitimate children left behind by the debauchery of white men. When she was young she had imagined her father as a different person, a journalist killed in the Middle East, a photographer lost in a South American jungle, or a priest who had succumbed to illness in Southeast Asia.

The situations in the Middle East or South

America were too complicated for her to decipher at her young age, so most of the time she stuck with her story of a priest. One time she was given a bible, and thereafter she claimed it was her father's, saying that it had been brought back from Southeast Asia by her father's fellow priests after his funeral. She also found herself a cross and told her classmates that her father had worn it to his last days. Being the daughter of a priest, she had to have been religious, so Evelyn studied the bilingual bible diligently and learned many stories from it.

But there was one thing that did not match her story, and that was her mother. Evelyn's mom had been the proprietress of the small general store near the market of their township for as long as Evelyn could remember, it was inherited from her grandparents. Everyday she was engaged in making up orders, taking delivered goods, putting them away or displaying them on shelves. She calculated money, negotiated prices with wholesalers, and persuaded customers to buy more than they needed. She shouted at delivery men making mistakes, passed on gossip to entertain customers, and confronted those trying to take advantage of her. Everything she did was absolutely normal, but none of it was like the wife of a priest.

Thus Evelyn never introduced her mother to her classmates. In fact, she avoided talking about her at all. Nor did she ever ask her mother about her father. Everything she knew about him she had overheard from their neighbors, her teachers, and the parents of her classmates. But there wasn't much information anyway.

Evelyn had been so afraid to talk about her family, it made each day at school a challenge. When other kids talked about their daddy, mommy, brothers and sisters, she had to apply her wildest imagination to make up what she had, because she had nothing. No father, no sibling, only a mother who she would mention as little as possible, she had to make up some relatives on her father's side in the US at some point. As young as she was, she knew a person must have a consistent personality, and he or she must not be one hundred percent nice or one hundred percent bad. There has to be some contradictory nature in a person. From storybooks she found in the school library, she borrowed some characters to be her remote family members.

Evelyn left home as early as she could. She was admitted to a quite prestigious senior high school in Taipei. Her mother's neighbors who were also her customers at the general store raised a scholarship for Evelyn to study in Taipei, because she was the first one in their neighborhood to go to such a top-notch school. In Taipei her foreign look seemed to be more accepted. Sometimes she was even asked to play a certain role in the school plays. She was glad to realize that among her fellow students, she was not the only one raised by a single parent.

Evelyn majored in English literature in college. With her look and her major, it was easy for her to work as an English tutor in cram schools, so she was able to support herself throughout her college career. She had several serious relationships, but none of them brought her close to marriage. After college, she worked as a translator or editor for publishing houses. She began getting involved in the copyright trade when Taiwan's publishing industry boomed in the 1990s, thanks to the abolition of Martial Law and the lifting of censorship.

These days Evelyn goes back to Tainan during holidays. It's the city of Taiwanese literature, although she knows American literature better. When she is not in her mother's store, she hangs around the second-hand bookstores. Old neighbors know her well; they were her education's sponsors. New customers find it odd to see a western face in such out-of-date stores. Tainan people have a particular nostalgia for old things; had her mother's store been established in another county, it would have been replaced by a 7-Eleven a long time ago.

Evelyn's meeting with Yu-Jin bothers her. She feels there is something she left behind since her childhood, but she is not clear what it is. She never had intimate conversations with her mother, like talks about her boyfriends or her career planning. But that is totally normal; Taiwanese young people do not necessarily share these things with their parents. But her mother is the only one she has in this world, and vice versa.

In April she goes back to Tainan for spring break. Her first morning home, she goes down to the store from their tiny living quarters on the second floor, and she stays to see if her mom needs any help. There is not much to do. The store sells cigarettes, beer, cooking wine, ramen, sundries and canned food. It hardly makes any profit, but it's a good place for old people to gather and exchange words.

Evelyn's mom has put on some weight in her later years, but she is still in good shape and handles everything on her own. Looking at her, Evelyn realizes she is actually a very beautiful woman, although as a little girl she thought her mom was vulgar compared to her teachers and the parents of her classmates. But watching her now, Evelyn thinks, what a glamorous old lady she is! Her Chiraya tribal blood gives her a radiant face, and her outfit, the decades-old dark green corduroy dress, is still in fashion today. She must be good at selecting her clothes and creating her own style. Why hadn't I ever noticed it before?

When her mom has finished her tasks of opening the store and moving several things to the arcade, she sits down in the chair under the arcade in the sunlight. Evelyn sits down next to her.

"Mom, you never talked about my father." Evelyn speaks in Taiwanese, a dialect she seldom uses.

Her mother looks at her, surprised, "Why do you ask about him now? You are not trying to track him down, are you? That only happens on TV shows."

Evelyn laughs out loud, "No, ha ha, it never occurred to me. I just wonder, what happened?" She explains to her mother that she had run into her childhood friend near her work and her blue eyes were the subject of a compliment.

"He was a beautiful man."

"How did you meet?"

"In this store. He came to buy ice cream."

"What's his name?"

"Julian."

Evelyn bursts into laughter, and her mother

squints her eyes at her, in doubt.

"He must be a blonde, right?"

"How do you know?" Mom's body twitches slightly. She is not very used to being questioned about this man who had faded from her life long time ago.

Evelyn does not answer; she has an amused mood now. They had a pet kitty called Julian when she was in elementary school. Julian had very light-colored hair. At certain times of the day, it really looked golden.

Julian was not exactly their pet: he was just hanging out with them, and sometimes taking food they offered. He was a cat that was so aloof that she sometimes considered him almost knightly.

In some ways, Julian really was her knight. When the parents of Evelyn's classmates came to collect their children after school, she was often accompanied by Julian only. It was impossible for her mom to leave the store around that time since parents tended to shop for things on their way home with their children. So Evelyn and Julian would walk together and play. Unlike other cats that chased rats or bugs, Julian never distracted himself with such loathful things. Their relaxed promenade would proceed, like two aristocrats patrolling their territory with pride. The less-than-ten-minute walk often extended into more than twenty minutes. Neither of them cared, nor did her mom.

When Evelyn left Tainan for senior high school in Taipei, Julian took his departure, according to Mom, without leaving any clue. Julian was someone loving and caring in their life for a significant period of time. He brought them warm memories, and that was all.

"Julian is a good name. What was his last name?"

"It sounds like Livensten, but I don't remember how to spell it. You are not going to search him online, are you?"

"Of course not! I just wonder if this guy really existed."

Her mom pinches her thigh, "Who do you think your flesh and blood are from?"

Evelyn is kind of surprised that her mom doesn't feel uncomfortable talking about this man. "I have been fatherless all my life."

"A lot of kids do well without a father. Actually, I believe a lot of kids do better if they don't have their father."

"True." But if Mom was so confident with their situation, why didn't they ever talk more about it before?

"It was an unlucky affair at two levels. First, he had to move back to America when the American military withdrew most of their troops from Taiwan. This all happened during the time when America decided to recognize China in the United Nations. Second, because Taiwan felt betrayed, there were quite a few anti-US protests everywhere when you were a little girl. You and I were naturally thought to be one of the consequences of American betrayal."

Evelyn's mother told her that a church provided her with a lot of assistance during that time, and she did need their support because as American troops left, their store business dropped significantly. "Especially the ice cream and ice bars."

Her mom explained that the economy of the township was badly shaken for it had relied on the activities of those American soldiers. "I could have got more support from the church. As a branch of the American Baptist Church in Taiwan, they felt obliged to take care of me. But in order to be one of them, I had to admit that what I had done was sinful, because in their minds a woman should never conduct premarital sex and have a child without the sacred vow of marriage."

Evelyn turns to look at her mother, who continues, "You were an annoying baby, a rebellious young girl, and you became a mystery when you entered adulthood. But you were never a mistake."

Evelyn feels she is on the verge of tears, but she refrains from crying. She wants to be as cool as her mother is.

"You were in love with this... Julian?"

"Looking back, I am not sure if we were in love or not. We hung out together a lot, but there were so many differences between us that needed to be resolved before we could work out our relationship. However, we were wonderful partners in dancing. He taught me modern dance, and I taught him our tribal dance. Julian wanted to be a dancer, but he couldn't afford to go to art school. He joined the military to save money for his plan to be a professional dancer. Julian was fascinated by Taiwanese indigenous dance. He even began to study their elements for choreography."

Her mother went on to explain that dancing together with all that physical contact brought them an overwhelming experience of intimacy, and they became lovers. "If I were an American girl, I would be praised as an independent, free thinker. But as a Taiwanese girl, I had to have been either a slut or a victim. Of course under the increasing resentment toward America throughout Taiwan, it was much easier to play the victim. When the American president went to China to shake hands with the communist leaders, the withdrawal of the American military victimized our whole town because business declined so badly. I still regret my victim role, not so much for myself but for the society I lived in, with its blind beliefs in certain virtues."

Evelyn is so surprised and proud to hear that. She now feels ashamed of herself. She had been hiding her mother from her teachers and classmates. She had believed that this woman was not elegant enough to be her imagined father's wife. Pride and shame, the twine of Evelyn's life.

"But how did you feel when you found out you were pregnant? Didn't you panic?"

"No. I tell you, daughter, despite the morning sickness, swelling limbs and mental storms caused by hormone changes, the pregnancy was the greatest blessing of my life. Becoming a mother is fun, great fun. It's not unlike dancing; a lot of things happen at the same time at different speeds. By no means can you practice or rehearse it, but that's the power of life, the power of giving life. Chiraya girls are taken care of by our ancestral spirits; one doesn't have to be afraid. Too bad that you were never interested."

Evelyn is stunned. For all her life she had been so careful not to conceive because she hadn't wanted to repeat her mother's mistake. It was true that looking through the eyes of others, she had understood her mother's having her as a misfortune. But her mother, this independent, free-thinking and regret-free dancer never considered a father to be a necessary condition for a woman to be a mother. Evelyn protests, "Now you are telling me it's fun. I am almost forty-five!"

"How could I know what was going on with you? Other girls figure it out in their twenties or thirties. I had no idea what was wrong with you."

"Were you ever in a relationship again?"

Her Mom shook her head, "Under the kind of anti-American climate that existed in Taiwan, we were the perfect evidence of American evils and were better left untouched. We received sympathy, and kindness was heaped on us, but our status was never to be changed."

Evelyn remembers that when she was in elementary school, the school had a movement "No American Products," where every school kid's household was supposed to stop buying anything from America. Protests were everywhere; people gathered in front of American institutions and smashed the car windows of American negotiators and representatives. Evelyn was not affected by the boycott at all since her mother could barely afford any American products anyway. Many years later when she and her classmates talked about it in college, she realized how useless the boycott was. The public restrained their desire to buy American food, American cigarettes, American sporting goods, and American appliances, but the entire island still heavily relied on the large machines imported from America for the manufacturing industry and construction. Most of the cars in Taiwan at that time were made in the US; even locally produced vehicles required American parts. Not to mention the chemicals and medicines that Taiwanese industries still were unable to produce. Nevertheless, the collective anger of a frustrated society became a blockage in her mother's life.

"We are the victims of nothing but false victimhood." Evelyn says.

"Huh?"

"Never mind."

They remain seated in front of the store; the sun is getting too warm now. A young man on a motorcycle stops in front of them, inquiring, "Do you have any Marlboros?"

"No!" The mother and the daughter answer in unison. The young man rides away.

First published by the Anthology of the 14th Conference of Short Stories in English:
West and East, Confluence and Influence, July 2016

First Lady

The First Lady ordered the president's office staff to engage a group of Russian experts to come secretly as soon as possible in reaction to the news that the local funeral home had reported that they could only preserve a dead body for a week at most. If long-term preservation of the corpse was a necessity, they suggested freezing the body or soaking it in a chemical solution.

"No. Mr. President must appear to be sleeping beside me."

Considering that Vladimir Lenin's body had been preserved for over half a century, the First Lady decided to consult the people who had taken care of Lenin's preservation.

In the conference room, the First Lady

learned, with the assistance of interpreters, that the solution of formaldehyde, methanol, ethanol, and a pH balancer mixed with a little bit of red dye had been injected into the veins at the back of the former Communist leader's neck right after his death to stop the decomposition. Under his suit there were two layers of rubber that made sure his body was always bathed in the special embalming fluid. Every two years they redid the embalming, a process which included bathing the body in several different solutions in turn, such as glycerol, potassium acetate, hydrogen peroxide, and sodium acetate.

The consultation and its prescription were costly, but the First Lady felt she had no other choice. The entire project took several months at the hands of five experts with several local people assisting them. During this time the First Lady held several meetings with the prime minister, who was the son of the president. In one meeting they talked about the replacement of the minister of interior.

"Is Mr. Yuanda a good choice?" The prime minister inquired carefully.

"He is, but Yuanda is obviously too fat for this position."

The prime minister was bewildered. A man's weight would affect his job?

"People expect to see a hard working public servant. Mr. Yuanda looks too well taken care of." The First Lady explained.

The prime minister agreed on this point and asked, "Is Mr. Kaimi suitable, then?" Kaimi was barely more than a skeleton.

"Mr. Kaimi is a respectable man, but... didn't he have an affair with his secretary?"

It was Kaimi who had competed against the prime minister for the chair of the National Security Council. He knew at that time that the only way to defeat Kaimi was to trap him with a sexual scandal. Sexual affairs do not destroy a man's political career, they just slow him down, and the prime minister knew that his government still needed Kaimi. He paid a young woman in Kaimi's office to seduce him; whether she had succeeded or not was of little concern, but they certainly would have been able to build up enough evidence for their purpose. Fortunately, Kaimi withdrew from the competition, so that fabricated materials were never used.

"Uh, it was just rumor...." Saying so, it dawned on the prime minister that the First Lady, who was also his stepmother, had a candidate in mind. He waited for her to speak up.

"Are you familiar with Mr. Laobuo?"

"Yes, yes. We worked together in the Hometown Beautification Program." The so-called "beautification" consisted of bulldozing slums and getting rid of beggars. Thereby the land could be yielded to developers to put up decent apartments, and government officials would share the under-the-table-bonus - in this government every project served multiple purposes. The prime minister then understood who was in the mind of the First Lady. There was gossip circulating that Laobuo's wife was her lesbian lover. But how it could be? After all, she "slept" beside the president every night, didn't she? The president was no longer able to verify it though. The prime minister couldn't help but squint as he focused his eyes on the rigid, waxy body of his father in the bedroom behind her.

"The new minister of the interior must be able to deal with the increasingly ferocious agitators nowadays," said the First Lady. The prime minister was clear that she was talking about those people demanding a direct presidential election process. They criticized that the representative system was subject to manipulation, which was, of course, quite true. The president had been in power for twenty-six years, re-elected by the National Assembly every six years according to the *Temporary Provision for the Period of National Mobilization*. Small turmoils were inevitable, but they were put to rest quickly, thanks to the nation's dense network of secret service agents and the tens of thousands of informants throughout the country.

"Mr. Laobuo is a perfect candidate." The prime minister consented, "What should be done with Mr. Pukiki?" Pukiki, the current minister of interior, probably knew his position was in danger since the president stopped appearing in public events. Of course, to the public, the president still worked hard in private with his cabinet; he had no time for public appearances according to the Central News Agency, a state owned institution.

"He will be the chairman of the National Land Planning & Development Foundation." The First Lady said. It meant that Pukiki would be able to pocket quite fat kick-backs from all kinds of public projects. Now he wished he were the one given the position; being the prime minister he was nothing but a courtier of Father and his wife. Had the First Lady known how lucrative the foundation was, she'd never have awarded the position to Pukiki, who was, in her eyes, an incompetent public speaker unable to guide public opinion, resulting in the spread of much unwanted information that led to troublesome activities. But who was able to control public opinion nowadays anyway? The influence from the West was greater and greater, uncensored publications were more and more accessible, and people absorbed different ideas easily. They no longer believed that social order and growth had to be sustained at the price of individual rights. Government achievements such as the full employment rate and the greatly improved infrastructure no longer entitled the rulers to conceal inconvenient truths.

Confining dissidents to prevent them from making trouble was increasingly difficult. In addition to a growing chorus of voices urging due legal process for every criminal charge, the government had to deal with "Human Rights Watchers" sent from the US or Europe. Perhaps it had been a mistake that the government had emphasized education so much. Farmers' children who went to college turned into spoiled brats. The "social equality" they never ceased talking about forced the government to face people from all levels: women, workers from the bottom of the society, and the disabled. It was really burdensome to attend their gatherings, visit their workplaces, and shake their hands. Why couldn't people be satisfied with what their leaders had done for them? Didn't their leaders deserve credit for the highways, schools, libraries and hospitals they had built? The democracy those so-called intellectuals were demanding only made progress impossible. How could the nation operate if everyone had a say in such highly professional, complicated matters?

"The new minister of interior also should

start drafting the laws for direct presidential elections." The First Lady said.

What? I am not going to succeed my father?! What a bitch. The prime minister couldn't find the words to protest.

"Of course we will do our best to help you run a campaign." The First Lady assured him.

That would be tough. People hated him; they hated him for being the president's son and being the prime minister. And he doubted that Laobuo would help him. What could go wrong if they just announced the death of the president and made him the successor? Even if a few dissidents would be certain to protest, so what? The prime minister, feeling bitterly disappointed, was dismissed by the First Lady.

In the following days the three newspapers covered the president's instructions for enacting laws to enable direct presidential elections, sidelined with the update of the new minister of interior who was appointed to be in charge of this historical task. The prime minister wondered how much longer the First Lady could continue this scheme. After all, even though their own people did not dare to question the long absence of the President from public occasions, foreign media would become suspicious.

Not that they were all just power thirsty, they also wanted to be able to step down and move to an "advanced country" to enjoy good weather and comfortable living. Nevertheless after decades of governing this nation and its troubled multitudes, members belonging to the ruling class had formed a symbiotic unity that meant no one could be left alone. Everyone was reliant upon the others and at the same time was extorted by the others. In order to bring the country forward, they all had to do a bit of dirty work. They had thought that once their national status improved and their development had reached the standards of the US or Japan, they'd stop. Unfortunately, the people had failed them. After almost half a century they were still far behind the US and Japan. Instead of working in step with the government guidelines for progress, the people cried out with all kinds of obscure demands that were irrelevant to the growth of their country.

One humid night in spring, the prime minister got a call from the First Lady, "Mr. president is sweating." They knew they had to take drastic measures quickly. The president's office called Moscow, unfortunately the Lenin Mausoleum was undergoing its bi-annual maintenance, so no one was available for consultation at that point. The prime minister rushed to his father's residence, and to his great regret, he saw the melting chunk of dead flesh with its rapidly deteriorating facial features. An abhorrent smell began to waft from the body. Neither of them knew what to do. Then all of a sudden, the earth quaked.

The next morning the headline of the major newspapers was, *Great Leader Passed Away During the Earthquake*. The story went that when the earthquake happened, the president's chauffeur drove the car onto the bridge, and their car, along with another eleven vehicles, was smashed under the weight of the bridge. Eight people had been killed, including the great leader. That was a convenient plot, the prime minister thought, and the bridge had served multiple purposes as well, including its fall.

The bridge had been constructed 14 years ago, as part of a project called the Ten Grand Constructions financed by the US. At that time the US was afraid that many smaller countries along the Pacific Rim would be absorbed by the Soviet Union, thus the US paid for many of their infrastructure works. The US also pressed these countries to improve their human rights records, for example, secret arrests were intolerable. Of course the demands were ignored, the US has no right to interfere in their domestic affairs.

They selected a contractor to design and construct the bridge. The mountains in the east contained rich cement ores, so several friends of the prime minister, as soon as he grabbed the political power, established a company to get hold of the mining rights, and the prime minister was given a substantial percentage of the shares in the company. Eversince the establishment of the cement company, all the public works, from design to construction, were encouraged to use as much concrete as possible. And because the cement company was almost a monopoly in the business, the price of cement remained high and the prime minister enjoyed a bulky bonus every year. Of course the cost of excessive concrete for the construction of the bridge had been compensated; the issuance of all kinds of licenses and permits had been waived.

In order to build the bridge, the largest span ever in the country that connected a harbor city in the north and a rising town in the south of a river, the slums on the two banks had been completely wiped out. So where had the poor people gone? Honestly speaking, the government did not care. Those were the uneducated, loathsome and jobless people who never paid taxes and never contributed to economic growth anyway.

The fall of the bridge made the prime minister suspect that in order to make up for the expense of using such large quantities of concrete, the contractor had most likely used as little steel reinforcement as possible.

Nevertheless, the prime minister thought, people killed by the fall of the bridge had been unlucky; but it was lucky that the bridge served multiple purposes, including its failure. Still, according to the *Guideline for Disaster Prevention and Mitigation*, the prime minister was obliged to explain the causes of the fall, he ordered the contractor to present a technological report of the damage.

The memorial service for the president was held two weeks later, and the funeral procession was miles long. The grieved but dignified widow of the great leader, in black suit and veil, won adoration from the news media. "How come people hate me as the son of the 'dictator,' but love her as his wife?" The prime minister was annoyed at the double standard.

Both the First Lady and the prime minister agreed to announce that the country was under a state of emergency and the direct presidential election had to be put off for a while. It was also natural under the circumstances that the prime minister would temporarily serve as the acting president. But to his surprise, the prime minister was informed by the president's office that, rather, the First Lady was going to be the official acting president during the emergency period. The prime minister rushed to the presidential residence and confronted his stepmother, who spoke not a word but handed him a pile of pictures. They were taken when he was with the woman he paid to seduce Kaimi. Although they had hung out together only to talk about their scheme, from the arrangement of the pictures, the dates, their outfits, their schedules of meeting and departures, as well as the lewd expressions on their faces, it could easily be made to look as if they had been dating each other frequently over a lengthy period of time. He has no idea how the First Lady got the photos and how did she see it. Was she the mastermind behind it, or was she made believe of the affair? After all, in this government, every project served multiple purposes.

By the time the prime minister left the presidential residence, he promised to endorse the First Lady as the acting president. It takes so many lies to operate this government, the prime minister thought to himself, and the power actually relied on the very strong willingness of everyone to believe the lies. The morality embraced by the public—a nation's leader must be austere and faithful—was shaped by the regime over the past decades, and everyone in the ruling class was, at least in the mass media, selfless with great vision, virtuous close to a saint. Those who rejected to accept the alternative reality and those who criticised the gullibility of the public were either discredited, or badly oppressed.

Back at his office, the prime minister told himself he should be positive about what the First Lady had used against him. An affair, true or not, was not meant to destroy him completely. He laughed to himself bitterly.

The report of the broken bridge was on his desk. He opened it and saw a picture of the First Lady at the inauguration ceremony. He immediately understood it to be a hint from the contractor that the First Lady was also involved in the construction, so a real investigation wouldn't do anyone good. The report attributed the failure of the structure mainly to the earthquake, naturally.

The prime minister sank into deep thought. Before completely giving up his hope to lead the nation, how could he have this project, a bridge which no longer existed, serve one more purpose?

First Published by Lunaris Review, Apr 2017

Wednesdays

Mourning is a mysterious thing. Mrs. Yeh doesn't know how to begin.

When her husband disappeared seventeen years ago, she wished that he had run away with his mistress, so she could hate him, she could stop worrying about him. She waited, but he never returned, and he never sent her any messages like he wanted a divorce or he was sorry. After four months had passed, she began to search for him. She went to places he liked to hang out, such as libraries, chess clubs, parks where he had sometimes taken walks, restaurants where he had often dined, but she found no trace of him. Maybe there were places he used to frequent that she didn't know about.

She had to call his friends and ask around, which was very embarrassing. What kind of wife was she, to have no control of her husband's whereabouts? She searched out phone numbers from any scraps of information that he had left behind, but even when she dialed all the numbers and uttered her plight to strangers, she still found nothing. Some people expressed their sympathy, but no one knew where Mr. Yeh could be.

Then one night a woman was waiting at her door when she returned home from work.

"I am Kao Ting-Pon's wife. Ting-Pon was taken away by police last March, and I was told he was with Mr. Yeh and Mr. Hu."

"What? What did they do?"

Seeing how surprised Mrs. Yeh was, Mrs. Kao was very troubled. She had hoped to glean some information from Mrs. Yeh, but she realized she had probably only brought the unknowing wife more pain. "They were... they probably have some friends who were involved with underground activities...." Mrs. Kao explained in a very obscure way.

"Illegal trade?" Mrs. Yeh looked so confused,

which only agonized Mrs. Kao even more.

"What have I done?" Mrs. Kao asked herself. She felt guilty for bringing up such upsetting news.

Seeing Mrs. Kao's hesitation, Mrs. Yeh said eagerly, "I've called and called, but no one knew where my husband was...."

"I was told they were taken to the Garrison Command first, then to a detention center in Liuzhangli. But what came next, I don't know." Both women were in tears.

Mr. Yeh was an anthropologist, he worked for a foundation connected with a university. A very curious and passionate man, Mr. Yeh liked to make friends from different professional fields. He organized reading groups, and there might have been some exchange of banned books, but many Taiwanese intellectuals possessed banned publications. How could one maintain intellectual integrity without challenging the stupidity of the censorship? Mr. Yeh's anti-government attitude was not a secret, but Mrs. Yeh couldn't imagine that her husband would have ever been directly involved in any anti-government activities.

So Mrs. Yeh paid a visit to the Liuzhangli Detention Center. Mrs. Yeh was a music teacher at Tongmen Elementary School, and she had no class on Wednesdays, so on Wednesday morning she took off for Liuzhangli. She had found out the location of the Detention Center previously; it took two bus rides and about a half hour walk.

The place was like a school from the appearance, only at the gate there were two military policemen guarding it with rifles. Mrs. Yeh was intimidated, but reflecting on how far she had come, she gathered the courage to approach one of them. "I am here to find my husband Yeh Jin-Long." She tried to repress the trembling in her voice.

"Which office does he work in?"

"No. He is not working here. He was... he might have been taken here...." Hearing this, the two policemen were ready to expel her from the premises.

"Please, ... I haven't heard from him for a long time...."

"Go! Go away! You can't be here."

"My husband was taken here. No matter what he has done, I must see him!" Without knowing the source of her courage, Mrs. Yeh lifted her voice. The one closer to her held his rifle higher. Mrs. Yeh stepped backward, but her fear transformed into anger. She stood firm, looking him in the eyes. The young man was in awe.

At this time a black sedan car drove toward the gate. Mrs. Yeh rushed over, trying to stop the car. The vehicle halted because now she was in its way. The military policeman stooped to say something to the person in the rear seat; then the window was rolled down. A man with oiled hair smiled at Mrs. Yeh, "Why don't you leave your phone number? We will check if Mr...."

"Yeh, Yeh Jin-Long, Yeh is like leaves, Jin is like gold, long is like dragon...."

"Yes, yes, Yeh Jin-Long, I will ask them to check if Mr. Yeh is here or not. Now please leave your phone number and go home. Once we have the answer we will call you. No civilian is allowed in this place." He rolled up his window as the car drove on and disappeared behind the gate. An assistant from the guard booth took out a piece of paper and a pen, so Mrs. Yeh wrote down her phone number. Just in case she was called when she was at work, Mrs. Yeh added the number of her office which she shared with five other teachers.

A week went by, but she never got a call. She thought of calling back, but the phone number of a detention center couldn't be found in the yellow pages.

Mrs. Yeh went again the next Wednesday. The military policemen at the gate were two different persons. She had to repeat her request with them, and when it did not work, she begged, "Sir, last week an official told me he was going to help. I just came to ask if there is any news about my husband."

"Who was the official?"

"I don't know, he was in a big black car…."

Hearing this, the gate guard said coldly, "Get out of here, this place is not for crazies like you!"

"Please, Sir, please check it for me. There might be some messages that were overlooked…."

The military policeman pointed his hand outward sternly, "Go!"

Mrs. Yeh did not know what to do. She walked away from the gate, but she still held onto hope that the car she stopped last week would show up again. She sat down on the concrete edge of the flowerbed by the wall opposite the detention center, so she could see if there was any vehicle passing the gate.

She sat there for hours until dusk.

For the following seventeen years she took every Wednesday off from school and came to sit there. Her situation was understood by her colleagues, and for some people it even became a symbol of courageous resistance against state violence. In the first several years, Mrs. Yeh was hopeful, then she was angry. Her anger was so tremendous that she never could let it go.

One winter morning, Mrs. Yeh got a phone call in her office. A woman's voice said, "Hu Young-Jen is released!"

"Who?"

"Hu Young-Jen." The phone connection ended.

Mrs. Yeh was reminded of the night when Mrs. Kao's wife told her that their husbands were arrested together with Mr. Hu. Now, seventeen years later, Mrs. Yeh spent the rest of her day unable to concentrate on her teaching, and once the bell of the last hour rang, she hurried home. She fished out all the materials that belonged to Mr. Yeh, all the stuff she had studied so thoroughly for years before giving up.

"Hu Young-Jen, Hu Young-Jen...." She murmured to herself while rummaging through the pieces of papers, afraid that she might miss something related to this person. She carefully turned the pages of Mr. Yeh's yellowed notebooks, embrittled phonebooks and aged calendars.

"There you go...." There was a Hu Young-Jen, along with his address, on the inner cover of a book of poetry. Mrs. Yeh felt her hands trembling. She realized she had actually met him a couple of times, and he had been invited by her husband to have dinner with them occasionally.

Of course the address was out of date. The city had been changed so much that the street was completely wiped out to make room for a subway station. Fortunately, the son of one of Mrs. Yeh's colleagues told her that a man on probation must report to his probation officer regularly. He told her he had inside connections, so he would try to find out for her who Hu Young-Jen's probation officer was.

After several weeks the young man found out where and when Hu Young-Jen was supposed to report to his probation officer, and he offered to accompany Mrs. Yeh if she wanted to approach Mr. Hu.

"No. It's very kind of you, but I think I am OK to do it myself." Mrs. Yeh was not even sure she would have the courage to talk to Hu Young-Jen.

Coincidentally, it was a Wednesday. Standing in the windy street outside of the probation office, Mrs. Yeh wondered how in the world she could tell which man was Hu Young-Jen. But then a man with a bent back and a walking stick turned up, and Mrs. Yeh was sure that he was Hu Young-Jen. She was surprised how old he looked, but she also realized immediately that she herself had also aged a lot. She wanted to turn away and run from the scene, but her legs were not under her control. She couldn't move.

As the old man walked toward the street, he came within speaking distance of Mrs. Yeh.
"Hu Young-Jen?" Her voice trembled so much. He stopped and looked at her, bewildered, and a flash of fear was in his eyes.

"I am Yeh Jin-Long's wife. Do you... do you know where my husband is?"

The old man was stunned. At first he waved

her away, and then he changed his mind and grasped her hands tightly. He was so agitated, he seemed to want to say something, but his breathing became so heavy, he couldn't utter any words. Mrs. Yeh took out a pen and a piece of paper. She wrote down her phone number and pressed it into Hu's palm, "Call me, please. Call me." Then she ran away as fast as she could.

Over the following weeks Mrs. Yeh's fear of getting a call from Hu was as great as her expectation. When he finally called, Mrs. Yeh suggested that she meet him in a park. She felt more secure in an open space. That afternoon they sat by the playground, where several kids were having fun under the watchful eyes of their parents or babysitters. Mr. and Mrs. Yeh did not have children; they did not have time to plan for it because Mr. Yeh disappeared in the fourth year of their marriage.

"We thought Jin-Long was released."

"Why?"

"The martial police told us he confessed and turned us in. The reward was his freedom."

"He never returned home."

Hu Young-Jen wanted to look at Mrs. Yeh, but he couldn't. He couldn't bear to look at her. For all these years he had thought Yeh Jin-Long was the only one spared by the cruel system of Garrison Command. He told himself not to carry the resentment of feeling betrayed and try to believe that his plight was not due to Yeh's confession. Now he has learned that his ambivalence for the past seventeen years was nonsense. But what had happened to Jing-Long?

"For what offense were the three of you charged?"

"We were accused of being spies of the Communist Party."

Mrs. Yeh lifted her eyes to stare at Hu, seeming to ask, "Were you?"

"We were just raising funds for a periodical published in Ann Arbor, Michigan, by a group of Taiwanese scholars."

"What was the periodical about?" Mrs. Yeh was so confused. How come people got arrested and put in jail simply for raising money for publications?

"It was to advocate democracy in Taiwan, demanding honest elections and transparent public policy-making."

Mrs. Yeh began to have a vague idea of what they did. They were the so called "dissidents," those people who criticized the government and called the president a dictator and a murderer. They said the ruling party cheated in every election, and the officials were corrupt. In the conservative society of Taiwan, voicing ideas like that was forbidden. She also vaguely knew, that almost everyone who said such things was considered a communist because they endangered societal peace and order.

"What happened to Kao Ting-Pon?"

"Executed. He was sentenced as the chief conspirator. My life was spared because I was only considered to be Kao's accomplice."

"You don't have any idea what happened to my husband?"

"I thought he was released. Mrs. Yeh...."

"No, he never returned."

Was it possible that Jing-Long would have hidden somewhere in order not to encumber his wife? But seventeen years? How could a man hide for seventeen years without contacting his agonized wife?

"I went to the Liuzhangli Detention Center every week over the past seventeen years, but they told me nothing."

"You what?!" Hu Young-Jen was appalled to hear that. For all the years he was confined, his parents, wife, children and siblings had been endlessly harassed by the law enforcement. The government fabricated all kinds of excuses to hassle them, checking their residence records from time to time, giving them a hard time when they were traveling, spreading vicious rumors to their social circles so they couldn't find jobs, couldn't make friends. They lived in fear, and the same torment was laid on Kao Ting-Pon's family, too. Why was Mrs. Yeh free from all the harassment?

Hu Young-Jen looked at Mrs. Yeh with nothing but great pain in his expression. There was only one explanation: Yeh Jin-Long had been removed. He had not existed since seventeen years ago, thus all the traces of this man must have been erased since then, that was why his wife was not under the state surveillance. It definitely was plausible, considering the kind of torture he had endured during the arraignment. Jin-Long was a man with a much smaller build than his; he couldn't possibly survive the torture that he himself had endured. And that was why Hu Young-Jen naturally believed the lies about Jin-Long's confession.

The hill at the back of the Liuzhangli Detention Center was known as a mass grave, and obviously it was where Jin-Long ended up. Hu Young-Jen bent his head down to his knees and began to cry. He cried and cried, like nothing could stop him. He cried for the horrible things that had happened to his brother-like friend, who shared his and Kao's ideals so much as to risk his life. He cried for his misunderstanding of his comrade, created by lies from the treacherous police. He cried for his best friend's widow who sought after him for seventeen years without any clue about what had happened. He cried for himself because he did not know how he should tell her the answer she had sought, knowing that she had spent the most precious time of her life in seeking it.

Seeing Hu cry so agitatedly, Mrs. Yeh gathered that her husband was dead. She wondered whether she wanted to know the details. She got up on her feet and walked, stumbling into the gusts of wind in early spring. What was the weather like the day when her husband and his two friends were taken away by the police? Were they handcuffed? What did he see and think at the last moment of his life? How much had he suffered? Did he regret what he had done?

The next Wednesday Mrs. Yeh began her mourning for her husband, formally to herself. After seventeen years she had finally become a widow. But mourning was a mysterious thing, Mrs. Yeh didn't know how to begin.

Those Healed and Unhealed

> *"And then, hemmed in as he is, he still always holds in his heart the sweet feeling of freedom, and that he can quit this prison whenever he likes."*
>
> ~ J. W. Goethe, The Sorrows of Young Werther
> (English translation by Burton Pike)

i.

Dr. Lin was almost ninety-years old, he had retired a long time ago, but for twenty years he maintained two outpatients clinics per week for his old patients, most of whom were his old friends. Today his friend Yang Qingchu was scheduled to visit. Yang was actually eighteen years younger than he was, they became friends because Yang was from Tainan and worked in Kaohsiung, and Dr. Lin was from Kaohsiung and went to school in Tainan. Both of them had been in jail.

Yang was a writer, he was working on his novel *Blackfoot Village* and he consulted Dr. Lin often. Dr. Lin had performed several amputations for patients suffering critical medical conditions around thirty years ago. Blackfoot meant the symptom of arsenic poisoning, due to the well water the patients had been accustomed to drinking for years. It had been a serious epidemic disease in the rural areas along the coast of Tainan and Kaohsiung during the 70s and 80s.

Today Yang brought his manuscript to Dr. Lin, in hopes that Dr. Lin would read it in case he made any mistakes on the medical terms. Dr. Lin was very impressed by Yang's diligent study of a topic he wasn't familiar with. He was reminded of the story Yang wrote many years ago about several girls working in a textile factory. He was amazed how clearly Yang described the production process of fabrics. When reading it, the entire workplace was vividly presented before his eyes. Dr. Lin was happy to know Yang's work was close to being finished and that his assistance had helped.

When Yang was about to take off Mr. Jiang rushed in, they almost bumped into each other. Mr. Jiang sat down, he came to have his right knee checked. Dr. Lin considered that this old man in his mid-eighties might be a lonely person for he tended to come for check-ups too often. But Mr. Jiang had family, he lived with his wife, and his children and grandchildren visited him from time to time. Assuring Mr. Jiang his knee was okay, Dr. Lin suspected that Mr. Jiang wished to chat more, so he asked how he was doing those days.

"I feel old...."

"Ha ha ha...." Dr. Lin laughed out loud, "You are telling me you feel old? I am four years older than you!"

"It's harder and harder to sleep normally now...." Mr. Jiang replied, dejectedly.

"Have you tried to take walks or some mild exercise?"

"No. Because I feel so old...."

"Force yourself a little bit. If it doesn't help, perhaps I can transfer you to the psychological clinic."

In order to divert Mr. Jiang's self-pity, Dr. Lin took his pen and wrote down "Factory Men" on a piece of paper, asking, "Do you know this book?"

"In fact, yes. Why?"

Dr. Lin was a little surprised because Taiwanese literary works were usually not familiar to the majority of the readers due to the repression of the Taiwanese dialect for decades.

"The man you almost bumped into just now is the author."

"What? Yang Qingchu? He has changed so much!"

Dr. Lin was more surprised that Mr. Jiang even knew the author in person. Mr. Jiang explained, "We were colleagues in the state-owned petroleum company."

Mr. Jiang seemed to want to say more about his relationship with Yang, but he hesitated. Dr. Lin waited. He was writing his memoir and was conducting a broad research of Taiwan's recent history. He liked to know more about Yang Qingchu whose literary achievements were a landmark in Taiwanese literature.

"In fact, I was the one obliged to watch him."

"You mean... the Second Office of Personnel?"

The Second Office of Personnel was in every governmental office and state-owned business, whose function was to make sure that every government employee was loyal to the nation. Dr. Lin knew Mr. Jiang had been the director of personnel in the petroleum company, but it never occurred to him that Mr. Jiang was in charge of such ugly business, for he was such a gentleman.

Unlike he and Yang who were local Taiwanese, Mr. Jiang was from Chinese mainland, the kind of elite that moved to Taiwan with the ruling party after the civil war in China. Mr. Jiang was well educated in China before the world war exploded. Mainlanders like Mr. Jiang were given quite privileged positions right after arriving in Taiwan even though they were so young and knew nothing about the business they were assigned. Looking back, Dr. Lin had no doubt that when they were given the jobs they were also ordered to conduct surveillance of their colleagues.

"The day before the Formosa Incident, I knew Yang was going to their congregation and I knew there would be arrests, so I sent him to Taipei to run some errands. But he took the night train to come back after he had completed his assignment."

Yang was arrested during the street demonstration for human rights and democracy in December 1979. The demonstration was defined as a riot because there were people of unknown identities mixed into the march initiated by the editors of *Formosa Magazine*, a banned journal at that time, and they started fighting halfway into their march. More than fifty of the protesters were arrested and tried as conspirators to disturb the social order. Yang Qingchu's depictions of people from the bottom of the society in his short stories gave the authorities the excuse to connect him with communism. He was sentenced and put in jail for more than four years.

"You tried to save him? Why?"

"He was such a talented young man, a really good writer. In order to write my report on him, I had to read all his works, at first I only tried to find criminal evidence, later I began to appreciate his achievement."

"Does he know that you had tried to get him away from the trouble?"

"I don't think so. Anyway, my effort did not work, he still got arrested."

"Were you worried that you might get yourself in trouble for helping him?"

"I did not think too much. I liked him very much, an unbending young man with idealism and passion."

"You, too. Mr. Jiang. What you have done was courageous."

Dr. Lin spent an even longer time in jail than Yang Qingchu. He was incarcerated on Green island for seven years. Dr. Lin had studied medicine in Japan when Taiwan was the colony of Japan. Later he practiced medicine in Manchuria, the colony of Japan in northeast China before World War II. When Taiwan was returned to China after the war, he continued his professional training in the medical school of National Taiwan University. He was very active in student affairs, and when he was a senior, he took the position as the chairman of the student association. He had no idea why he and several of his fellow students were arrested and put in jail. He heard there were arrests of communist spies or separatists in order to stabilize the ruling power, but he was not one of them. Being an intern in the hospital, he exhausted himself everyday by studying, taking care of patients and doing the most trivial tasks for senior doctors, how could he have time to involve in political activities? Decades later, when martial law was abolished, censorship lifted, surveillance stopped and government archives released, he learned that the ruling party was especially sensitive to student movements, because that was how the Communist Party rose to power in China.

He was lucky enough to survive at all. After he was released from the offshore prison on Green Island, he was told that quite a few of his fellow students were executed right away without trial. Chiang Kai-Shek's policy of maintaining a stable power was "rather to kill 99 innocent than to miss 1 guilty". Human lives were nothing to the status and power of the regime.

A little past noon, Dr. Lin closed the windows and doors of his clinic and carefully put Yang's manuscript into his suitcase. He couldn't wait to read it.

Yang Qingchu's novel *Blackfoot Village* would be published by the Cultural Bureau of Tainan, his hometown. It was a great honor for a writer to have the government as his publisher. Yang deserved it not only because of his outstanding literary skill, but also because of his courage and passion in pursuing art of the highest form. Dr. Lin told himself to focus on improving his own writing by using Yang's style as a model.

ii.

Just as Dr. Lin began to assume that Mr. Jiang's situation must have improved as he hadn't come to the clinic for quite some time, Mr. Jiang turned up again.

"I want to tell you something." Mr. Jiang spoke with a serious look. Dr. Lin wondered what he was going to say. Had Mr. Jiang been diagnosed with some incurable disease? After all he was eighty-five years old.

In the antique but tidy clinic, Mr. Jiang brought Dr. Lin back to 1950, the year that had decided Dr. Lin's fate.

iii.

It was the second year since we'd moved to Taiwan with the military. Here we would prepare to fight again and take back Chinese mainland from the Communist Party, the horde of bandits who killed or persecuted people and showed no respect to good old Chinese traditions. They overturned my hometown, all the villagers, including my parents and my brothers were forced to run. I was the only one who came to Taiwan and having no idea as to the whereabouts of any of my family. The only way to find them and to avenge them was to reform the Nationalist Party and strengthen Taiwan, the Free China, into a fortress of anti-communism.

I was a second lieutenant in the army, and after we retreated I was told the government no longer needed so many troops, so I retired, although I did not understand why fewer troops were maintained when we were planning to fight back. Anyway, I was lucky to be given a not bad job. It was a better deal compared to most of the low ranking soldiers who became jobless once they arrived in Taiwan. I started working in the administration of National Taiwan University, the former branch of the Tokyo Imperial University. I was happy to be able to continue my education that the war had put to a halt. This job was perfect. I was twenty-six years old, only a few years older than a college student.

Then we faced a very sinister situation: communist spies and conspirators who intended to shake the government of Free China in Taiwan. Each of us was assigned to watch several people around us to find out if they were absorbed by the Communist Party. I did my duty diligently by keeping an eye on the three men my superiors thought needed to be investigated. I wrote reports about them noting nothing of interest when I felt there was nothing wrong with them, but my superiors told me my work was not complete yet. Obeying orders, I spent more time following them which took all my time away from attending the classes in the University. But that was not the worst of it.

One day a colleague told me that he was ordered by the Second Office of Personnel to turn in at least one person under his watch. We had served in the same unit in the army and we were in each other's confidence for such highly sensitive matters.

"I am not trained to be a secret agent or to do stake-outs, how can I find out who are the good people and who are the bad people?"

"I understand. People criticizing public business are not necessarily conspiring to disturb the government." I expressed my sympathy.

"Right. Evil people don't manifest their evil intentions. Otherwise they won't shout out loud."

"This net of surveillance has a hole. You might be framed if you have a problem with your co-workers or neighbors. I heard a man lost money in gambling and he reported the winner, accusing him of being a communist spy."

"This whole thing has gone weird. How can I know whether a college lecturer of philosophy is a spy or whether a resident physician is?"

"What'd happen if you tell the Second Office of Personnel that both of them are innocent?" I inquired.

"I myself will be in trouble."

We used A and B to discuss the two persons,

the former was a scholar from poor farming parents, a cynical thinker and very hard to get along with. The later was from an elite family and well bred, and a hard-working caregiver.

So I told my friend that the young man from a prestigious family would have better chance to get away from the sick political system....

iv.

Without a doubt the young man was Dr. Lin. Memories of confusion, loss and pain surged up to Dr. Lin's head like a seastorm.

Seven years, seven years in the murky prison without knowing what he had done to cause his ordeal and whether he would be executed or released, that was the "better chance" Mr. Jiang had assumed? How many days he'd sat in the prison with his mind emptying out little by little until he lost count of time? What was the purpose of counting time for a life without a future anyway? How many times had he told himself that he must end everything as long as he still could feel at all?

No one in his family was able to mention his name, because people were afraid to show any friendliness to the family of a communist spy. Since his arrest, he stopped existing, and even after he finally was released, he couldn't recover his dignity because of the obscure shame and fear of his family. He couldn't be with his father when he was dying, he was absent when his little sister got married. They hid their thoughts from him, and hushed their conversations when he was around.

It took him four years to regain his professional status, and a lot more time to win trust from his colleagues. In order to be able to practice medicine, he had to endure all kinds of insults from some of his peers when promotion was at stake. That was the "better chance" Mr. Jiang had assumed based on his friend's oversimplified profiling of him?

The clinic fell into silence. Both old men could have been suffocated by it. The sunlight seemed to stop moving for a long moment, their eyes were dazzled. Mr. Jiang eventually gathered enough strength to stand up and stumble toward the door. After all it was not a coincidence that Mr. Jiang was his patient, Dr. Lin told himself. Was there ever any true trust between the doctor and the patient?

In the following weeks Dr. Lin felt unsettled. He had to admit that what he had believed to be left behind was still haunting him. The five decades of being a free man never could make up for his trauma. And monetary compensation or legal redress from the government after the fact of having spent years in prison was nothing compared to the horror, despair and hopelessness he and his family had experienced.

He wished Mr. Jiang had never told him the truth.

Before Chinese New Year, Yang Qingchu stopped by to deliver his new novel. He placed two copies on Dr. Lin's desk. The covers and layout of the inner pages were impressively designed. Dr. Lin was proud of Yang.

"Have you ever imagined your fate might be different if you were not in the demonstration in 1979?" Dr. Lin asked Yang curiously. Yang started writing *Blackfoot Village* as early as in the 1980s, if he had not been a political prisoner, he might have published it long time ago.

"I've imagined everything but then I finally dropped the ideas that my life could have been better or worse. It's useless brainstorming and it never relieved my pain. Nothing can be changed by anything." Yang smiled. Dr. Lin didn't know whether or not to share the stories Mr. Jiang had told him with Yang. He didn't want to make Yang feel how he had felt over the past weeks.

Then Yang's mobile phone rang, he said to Dr. Lin before answering it, "You are a doctor, you fix things and heal people as well as you can, but by no means can you heal historical traumas. Leave the scars as they are so your mind will be freed." He pressed the bottom of his mobile phone and spoke loudly: "Say hi to Dr. Lin, my dear." A female voice could be heard from the small machine speaking delightedly, "Dr. Lin, long time no see!"

"Now I am leaving for my date with my daughter." Briskly Yang walked out while talking to the phone, the sunlight was back on his face.

Dr. Lin spent several days reorganizing his old stuff, things he used when he was a medical student, papers from the authorities when he was confined and letters he wrote to his family that he never could mail to them. Then there were the certificates of his profession, and notes after notes of his own research for his writing, medical papers or memoirs. Yang's words re-emerged in his head from time to time.

He unfolded a letter he wrote to her sister:
Dear Hui:

Your letter did not arrive until yesterday, it took 5 weeks. But I am so excited that it arrived at all. I read it many times, it brings me a lot of comfort. I am glad to know you like biology. Biology was also my favorite subject when I was in high school. Do you have a microscope? I used to picking up everything and slice them so I could observe them with it. You'd be amazed by the brilliance of the micro world.

Biology will open a door for you to many

things, such as entomology, zoology, botany, bacteriology, virology and medicine... of course you don't have to be an expert of any of these fields. Here I draw a bug I found on my windowsill for you. Saying this, it's probably nice to be a biological illustrator, too.

I hope to get more of your letters, telling me how you are doing. I miss you very much and hope I will be coming home soon. I remember German writer J.W. Goethe had written in his novel "The Sorrows of Young Werther" that Werther feels the urge to cut open his own veins so he would be able to breathe and enjoy the eternal freedom. I feel the same way. I regret I can't help you more with your homework, but my best friend Yeh Sheng-Ji in medical college is really good in biology, and his math is also good, if you need a tutor, I am sure he will be happy to help.

This letter was sent and returned, he did not know why. Perhaps it was because his family did not want her sister to write him more as he requested, for his little sister never was clearly told why her brother was away and couldn't come home. The second possible reason was, *The Sorrow of Young Werther* was banned in Taiwan at that time for the suicidal content. But the most likely reason was, after he was released in 1957, he learned that his best friend Yeh Sheng-Ji was arrested and killed about the same time as his arrest, so the letter never passed the checking of the prison.

Holding the letter, Dr. Lin's hands trembled so much. His little sister passed away several years ago, throughout her life she maintained a distanced respect for her brother. Dr. Lin had no doubt that she had been repeatedly warned not to stay close to him since she was a teenager and by the time his name was finally cleared decades later, they were strangers without knowing much about each other's personal history. He barely saw her children, and she probably did not know much about his.

"Leave the scars as they are so your mind will be freed." He had put too much effort into correcting things like a surgeon cutting off the tissues that had gone bad. Yang's insightful words reminded him that he was in denial about the unhealed past—it could not be healed.

Mr. Jiang had done the right thing with a noble intention, and his confession was even a courageous thing to do because he let Dr. Lin decide whether he would be forgiven or not. But Dr. Lin was not in the position to forgive or not to forgive Mr. Jiang. After all, they were all victims whether they were inside or outside the concrete prison. Imagine the torment Mr. Jiang had given himself all those years returning to his clinic so frequently, Dr. Lin reflected.

A gust of wind blew in from the open window, it was about to rain. The first rain of spring. It was late in the night, long past the time Dr. Lin usually went to bed. He stood up from his desk and put out the lamp, deciding that the first thing in the morning he would call Mr. Jiang.

Impossible to Swallow

Phil heard Abilene in the next room yelling at the people from the trading department, "We are a research team. We don't give trading orders; we give suggestions. We don't tell you what to do! Traders trade with their own brains! How dare you put the responsibility on me. Your department isn't ruined by a few linguistic errors. You have tons of reference material, so reference!" The other people in the room were shouting back, but they must have been on the far side because Phil did not hear them as clearly as he heard Abilene.

Then Abilene raised her voice again, "No, it's not a mistake made by a foreigner; it's simply an incorrect copy of a few words out of millions of pages, I am sure there are other errors, but we get blamed whenever your people make mistakes, and once again you want to scapegoat one of my people!" After using Chinese to argue for a moment, she added, "No, no one is considered unqualified in my office for failing to understand Chinese. You guys trade in Dubai as well; do you trade in Arabic? Don't you rely on information presented to you in languages you understand?" When she spoke at the top of her voice, her accent seemed to lighten her English.

Hearing this, Phil knew his ass was saved, although he assumed that from now on his days in this company would be harder. But in the following several days Abilene did not make it any harder on him; his life was just as difficult as it always had been. In the weekend work meeting, Abilene just mentioned casually to everybody, "If there is anything you are not one hundred percent sure of, ask your colleagues. It's not something to be ashamed of." Phil and everyone present, he supposed, realized what she meant. In one email Phil had mistakenly translated the Chinese words "upper limit" into "lower limit" because he confused the Chinese characters "Up" and "Down." Because of his mistake, the trading office made a transaction that cost them millions of dollars in one morning.

***

Daphne was so scared. She closed her Facebook page so her friends, whether they supported the strike or not, would not leave any message. She didn't even want her relatives, classmates or friends to know she was working for the airline.

She started working as a flight attendant for the airline two years and nine months ago. To many, it was an enviable job. Flight attendants for most of the Asian airlines are required to be young, nice-looking, tall and strong enough to help passengers with their luggage, and able to speak English fluently. It's almost like the requirements for fashion models. The pay for flight attendants had been reduced over the past two decades, but compared to how much her classmates were making as engineers or teachers, or editors, or travel guides, her income was still significantly higher.

Their uniforms were very tight skirts, and except during the flights when they were delivering meals, for most services they were asked to wear high heels. This had become a tradition. She knew about it when she applied for the job, but recently their working conditions were getting worse and worse. The administration changed the method of calculating their working hours and benefits, and their number of flights suddenly increased without corresponding compensation. And as more and more flights were taking off after midnight to compete with the airlines from the Middle East which joined the market recently, she began to hear whispers about a protest, even a strike.

At first she pretended she did not hear it, she wished she could get over the exhausting new schedule eventually. But, no, she had been asked to take the places of her colleagues more and more often because some of them quit, some of them took leaves for not being able to meet the increasingly impossible schedules. Then one day she got called from one of her colleagues, telling her their union was organizing a strike. Her first response was that she wished she did not answer the phone call, she wished she could stay out of it. But if everyone stayed out, how could they have the bargaining power to negotiate with the administration?

She and her boyfriend just bought an apartment in the suburbs of Taipei and planned to get married in a couple of years, she needed a stable income. What if she lost her job? A job as a clerk in any business would not make enough money to pay off their mortgage.

***

Abilene was a single Taiwanese woman in her early forties, and she was also Phil's immediate supervisor in this office—the research department of the Taipei branch of a Dutch securities firm. Their work covered the markets of Taiwan, Hong Kong and China. People working for this company came from all over the world, so multilingualism was just fundamental. Many of them spoke three, even four languages.

Chinese and English were the most commonly used languages, but when the local staff didn't want foreigners to hear their conversations, they used Taiwanese. Abilene had a pet phrase, "impossible to swallow." At first Phil was confused as to what she meant by that, for it could be referring to bad food, or a result of tension or conflict, or sometimes it sounded like a vow to do something. Later he realized it actually came from the Taiwanese language.

Phil came from the US and was thirty years old. He got this job by, basically, boasting about his language skills. That had been his lifetime strategy, exaggerating how good he was, then making it up as soon as possible once he was offered what he sought. It brought him his Ivy League degree and several jobs resulting from short-term projects of sub-organizations of the United Nations. He had traveled extensively and seen many parts of this world, and he thought working overseas would be a cool thing. Phil had believed that working in a relatively less developed and exotic country like Taiwan was even cooler. But this job had become so demanding, every day he returned home exhausted, without the time or energy to pick up Chinese at all. The consequence was his confusion between "Up" and "Down" in Chinese characters.

Around the Lunar Chinese New Year two years ago, Phil was notified that he was being offered a job in this company, and that he should start right after the holidays. His future colleagues were also informed about his coming, so they sent him an email greeting, inviting him to spend the New Year with Abilene's family in Chiayi, her hometown. Phil accepted the invitation immediately; he was excited to see how people spent Chinese New Years in rural Taiwan. They picked him up at a subway station in Taipei and drove south in the crazy holiday traffic.

His companions were Abilene, Molly, and Jason. At first Phil thought Molly was his future boss, since she was educated in Australia and spoke perfect English. Jason was younger than the two women, and his role as a male was no different from Abilene and Molly. They seemed to do everything by themselves, even carrying or moving heavy stuff.

In the farming village, Phil was appalled to see how shabby Abilene's parents' home was. The structure was patched with cheap materials such as brick, concrete slabs, and plastic panels. The roof was corrugated iron. Inside the house, however, it was surprisingly tidy, although every piece of furniture seemed to be centuries old.

When they were introducing Phil to the tropical fruit trees they grew, Abilene saw someone at the other end of the orchard. She immediately changed her city shoes into a pair of rubber boots and walked into the muddy farmland. Jason explained to Phil, "That's her great uncle."

When she had finished her greeting and walked back, Phil couldn't help but squint at her muddy boots. To his horror, he saw a long earthworm crawling beside her feet. He knew it was totally natural in this place, but he turned his head away and tried not to think about it.

Abilene's parents were very quiet. During the New Year Eve dinner they hardly spoke, even though all the delicious dishes had been prepared by them. After dinner Phil expected to see them burn paper money and incense to worship local gods and ancestors, but they did not. "We are Christians." Abilene said. What a shock for Phil, to experience a humble farming family who were not believers of local deities but followers of Jesus.

***

The atmosphere in the work became weird since Daphne got the phone call. She felt everyone was cautious in interacting with one another. Are they for the strike or against the strike? She kept raising the question to herself and dared not really ask anyone.

The following weeks turned ugly. When the news of the pending strike was revealed, she heard all kinds of criticism. The strikers were called greedy brainless women with no skill but appearing makeup. She knew a lot of people thought flight attendants were no more worthy than waitresses, and waitresses in Taiwan were deemed the least skillful people who took the minimum hourly wage. Was the public aware at all that their works were much more than just serving drinks and meals? She knew even waiting tables could be a tougher task than people thought, still, she realized her pride was hurt being compared to a waitress.

She felt so thankful when her colleagues clearly explained how their new working schedules had shortened the time they needed to rest and adjust to jet lag to the public in order to win more support. For example, flying from Taipei to Los Angeles took twelve and half hours, and their resting time was counted half hour after the aircraft has landed, and after ten hours, they should be ready to fly again. Half hour after landing most of the passengers would be still in the aircraft, and their company assumed they were off duty already. And even after they left the airport and checked in the hotel nearest to the airport, they would have fewer than seven hours for sleep, and sleep should not be the only thing they could do between shifts. One had to be a robot to meet such workloads and schedules.

***

The first week of his work, Abilene asked Phil to present a report on the yield curves of Taiwan's government bonds in terms of two-year, five-year, ten-year, and twenty-year yields. They wanted to see the trends and the impact on Taiwan's financial industry. Never really having worked in financial business before, Phil barely knew how to make charts of yield curves. He spent several days and nights copying, past-ing, and google translating what he found online, and he finally turned in a four-page paper with a chart on the last page. When Abilene took it, she skipped the first three pages that Phil had spent a lot of energy to put together, and turned directly to the chart. Immediately she said, "This can't be right." She lifted her head, asking, "Phil, what was your major in college?"

"International Relations," Phil added eagerly, "but I have an MBA from Dartmouth!"

"I know that." Abilene called Jason in and asked him to help Phil check his data again.

Phil followed Jason to his desk and said annoyedly, "How does she know it's not right just by glancing at it?"

"We have been watching it all the time, so we know what the curves must look like. Molly and I are compiling the paper about risks. Together we will be able to analyze what shape Taiwan's bank industry is in. In this office we use a lot of mathematics."

Jason introduced Phil to several websites where they retrieved data, "Most of them have an English version ready, but if you find something interesting, and you can't find it in English, you can always ask assistants for help. But it takes more time. In this business, everything is a race."

Over the next two years whenever Phil felt his paper was good enough to turn in, Abilene would ask him to add some parameters. As he did so, his models and formulae grew bigger and more complicated. At the same time, the total number of papers he submitted became much fewer than he had planned.

***

At first Daphne got endless calls from people at her airline, some tried to dissuade her from participating in the strike, some expressed their concern for their jobs, and some advised her what to do, such as how to win more support from the public, and how to organize people and things once they needed to stay in the streets for more than one week.

Of course there were also phone calls not without threats, and she did get worried whenever getting messages like that. But did she have choice? The working conditions were so bad that she and her fellow flight attendants hardly had any personal life if they wanted to remain employed. But tons of comments under each of the online news articles about the strike said if they were not happy they should just quit and look for other jobs. She hated the sourness contained in such comments; the administration screwed it and she and her colleagues were supposed to go? That's so unfair. And she also saw that usually people criticizing them were those who had no better working conditions, they talked about how their situations were twisted and how they swallowed it and survived. It surprised her. Shouldn't people suffering from being exploited stand together to fight instead of tolerating the worsening conditions they were given?

Then the image of their union became to be discredited in the mass media. One of their high ranked administrators even said to the reporters that the union was kidnapped by a few people who rejected rational negotiation.

So her colleagues had to make a list of the past efforts they had tried for so long but which had been completely ignored by the administrations reports to the news media. Then veterans of environmental protection, human right watching or anti-globalization activism told them that stigmatizing the protesting groups was a typical trick, there was no different whether they were for their own welfare, working conditions, or for the environment, for human right, or against globalization. They were also told to be prepared for the shitdigging of their private lives, especially the leaders of the strike.

Daphne's mind was blown by their analysis of the street movements in the past. That was the politics she had always avoided to hear, to discuss, not to mention to getting herself involved. Only if she could have stayed the way she was.

From the TV news a chairman of a large chain convenience stores said, flight attendants on the strike would certainly lose their jobs and would not be hired by any other corporation. Now she was less scared by such remarks. She knew the chairman was kind of speaking to his own employees in case they demanded more from his own business. She had great fun when his talk only infuriated more people, and some activists pointed out that it was the evidence of the worsening problems of the employers of large corporations all over the world.

***

Now, just after Thanksgiving, Abilene announced that she was retiring, and Phil seemed to be the only one surprised in the office. Abilene was only forty-four, and as a vice president of a European securities firm, she made good money and could be promoted and earn even more in the future. Why would she retire now? Abilene told them she was going back home to help her parents with their farming, and Phil found that hard to believe. If his friends back in the US had achieved as much as Abilene, they'd buy bigger houses, drive fancier cars or start collecting artworks. And Abilene was going back to the poor village to be a farmer?

At the same time Abilene sent Phil to a meeting in London right before Christmas to present their strategies in serving a Taiwanese appliance manufacturer to issue overseas corporate bonds in order to enter British and European markets. Why not Molly or Jason, or anyone senior? Phil asked, and they said it was a relatively small business, and, "You speak better 'English', it's your job to deal with 'English'".

"No, in fact, I speak American." They laughed, although Phil felt nervous representing his business for the first time.

"After the meeting, you can fly back to the East Coast for Christmas." Abilene said. That was a bonus, because although there would be no trading during the Christmas holidays, Christmas was not a national holiday in Taiwan and all his colleagues would be still in work.

Abilene and Jason helped Phil prepare his presentation, and during their small talks Phil vaguely suspected that he was sent to the meeting mainly because the Taiwanese team did not like the clients they were dealing with in London. It's an ancient strategy of war, "matching your weakest team with the best of your opponents, and your best their second best, your second best their weakest." Phil was pissed at first realizing it, but on the other hand he did feel Abilene and Jason working so hard to assist him and he learned a lot more than his usual working days. He also knew that, part of his mission was to explain the differences of corporate governance in Taiwan and in the West due to the very different Asian culture, and why their clients should not expect things as they expected from other businesses they were familiar with.

***

On December 18th their strike organizers announced that the strike would start at midnight. Daphne and several of her colleagues who were not on duty the night before brought yoga pads, sleeping bags, water and food to the headquarters of their airline for vigil. She was surprised that as the night dragged on, more and more people gathered there to express their support. They said it would be a historical incident that the oppressed workers finally could have a systematic protest which never ever could happen in the history of Taiwan before, thanks to the legacy of previous social movements in even more difficult times, as well as the solidarity of the union's nearly three thousand members.

But the dramas were staged at the airport. As the airline had to cancel more than sixty flights in the next day, travelers arriving at the airport realized that they couldn't fly and began to shout to the ground staff. Some blamed the flight attendants, calling them self-centered, some pointed out that the administrators should be responsible for their inconvenience. The check-in counters of the airline became a circus ground, travelers with luggage scattered around, not knowing whether they should wait or should find tickets from other airlines, or go home. From the TV news she saw the ground staff bow to the angry travelers to apologize again and again. It was hard to watch, she wished they had their own union, too. The CEO of their airline swore that everyone on strike would be fired and sued. The spokesman of the union expressed their regret that the administration had no intention to solve the problem and the strike certainly would continue had the attitude of the high ranking executives maintained like this. He also pointed out that, the union has been dealing with such an attitude for years and now the public finally was able to witness it.

In the early morning, in the airport, Phil, with his luggage for the meetings in the UK and vacation back at home in the States, helplessly stood among the disappointed, angered, or desperate travelers. He had called Jason and Jason called other airlines to find tickets for him, but of course any substitute ticket had been taken. Finally they had to call London to inform their clients that the meeting was not going to happen. Phil was distressed, his Christmas break just burst with his opportunity to impress the clients in London.

***

Abilene's moving day was scheduled a couple of days before Christmas, when all of the West began its holiday time. Out of curiosity, Phil volunteered to help her move. Since she still was coming back to Taipei from time to time, most of the stuff she packed were her books from her apartment. Before putting them into boxes, Abilene briefly introduced Phil to what kinds of books they were. Many of them were in Taiwanese, mostly very old and tattered, with the yellowed pages embrittled. Some of them smelled weird. One of them was a bible, and many of the words were spelled with English letters to represent the sounds. Phil had had no idea that written Taiwanese was different from Mandarin.

"We lost a lot of this language." Abilene explained how previously Taiwanese had been banned from use in schools or on formal occasions. "That's why I use Taiwanese as much as I can, in case one day I forget how to speak my mother tongue."

"I thought you spoke Taiwanese in order to exclude foreigners like me."

"That's another reason, too." They both laughed out loud.

On their ride to Chiayi, Abilene told Phil more about her family. Her parents had been victims of the White Terror for drafting a statement of human rights through a presbyterian church in the 1970s.

"What's the White Terror?"

"A terrible repression of freedom of speech, where everything was under censorship."

Born and raised in the US, it was hard for Phil to imagine what it could be like to live without freedom of speech, a right guaranteed by the First Amendment… the first, not the second or third. Freedom of speech was as natural as air to Americans.

"What obstacles were there for demanding human rights then?"

"Too many things had be operated secretly in the name of national security, and if they were examined, the faults, collusion and corruption of the ruling power would be shaken. Expressing opinions freely, asking for democracy and transparent decision-making, criticizing the government without fear of persecution—those were rights that the regime couldn't afford to give to the people."

"What role did the church play?"

"At first the activists thought that the political powers wouldn't interfere with the church, and that the international connection between churches would pressure the government not to touch them. They were wrong. Their church was searched, and more than two thousand copies of Taiwanese bibles were confiscated."

"Why? Why confiscate bibles in Taiwanese?"

"They were used as evidence of separatism, for the independence of Taiwan."

Abilene explained that a bunch of people were arrested, and her dad disappeared for nine months. When he finally was released by the Secret Service, he became a completely different man. He retreated to the small village and became extremely quiet.

"We never knew what happened during the nine months of his incarceration, and ever since that time my entire family had been under surveillance. Law enforcement hassled us from time to time."

"In order to survive he had to give up his activism, I suppose."

"He did not, though. We knew he always

worked with his friends secretly. After the failure to launch a statement publicly, they knew their work must be accomplished underground."

"Wow! That's courageous...."

"They have God."

"But God failed them. Their tasks were aborted and they suffered!"

"If there is more to accomplish in the future, God is allowed a failure."

Phil turned to look at Abilene's profile, inquiring carefully, "Do you really believe that?"

"No." Abilene replied without any hesitation. They laughed out loud together.

With her eyes focusing on the road ahead, Abilene said, "Sometimes our inexplicable faith makes us believe we can endure greater hardship, so we are enabled to make noble decisions."

"If it was me, I would have given up and

stayed down, speaking and writing only harmless things."

"I believe my parents considered that, too, but the situation did not allow for it. Censorship is not like setting a boundary between what you can express and what you cannot. It operates together with fear, distrust, and hatred, like a web repressively entangling and tightening your mind all the time. Your life gradually erodes, until...."

"... it's impossible to swallow." Phil found the words that Abilene failed to grasp.

"Exactly."

***

Three o'clock in the morning. The number of people gathering in front of the airline's headquarters increased steadily. Tents were set up, bottled water and food were delivered. Together with the banners they had manufactured, she realized that to the activists of many social issues, what they were doing was nothing different to a street movement. The flight attendants on strike represented all the laborers needing to improve their working conditions.

Their strikes made the headlines of every news media in Taiwan. She never thought of it. She never thought of herself being equal to the workers from the factories shut down because of the WTO, or the highway toll collectors losing their jobs after the system of electronic toll collection was adopted, or the students occupying the parliament to terminate the free trade agreement with China.

Dozing during the vigil, Daphne dreamed of herself flying to London again. She liked the city very much, she wished she would have more time to see it. The strike must succeed, the strike must succeed, she murmured. She did not want to just sleep her time in London away, but the time for rest was so short that she was going to miss it again....

"Stay with us, Stand with us...." Her colleagues were singing to fend off the sleepiness. Cups of coffee were passed around. Was that how those laid-off factory workers were doing during their days, even weeks of street protests? It was the first time in life Daphne felt she was taking risks beyond her control, on the other hand she felt she was protected, by her colleagues as well as those strangers surrounding them.

She must have slipped into sleep on the cardboard ground when rain dropped on her face. Protestors began to move toward the canopies of buildings or tents set up earlier for them. Light ponchos were passed around. When the rain became really heavy, the union leaders announced that they should go home and come back at 9 pm since the negotiation had kicked off. Damp and tired, Daphne agreed it was a good idea.

***

After three and a half hours driving, they arrived in Abilene's hometown. As Phil was helping her unpack the boxes of books, arranging them on shelves which were roughly made of bricks and wooden panels, he felt Abilene's father's gaze. He could hardly conceal his agitation.

Touching each book carefully, Abilene told Phil, "I rescued these books when I was barely a teenager. At one point the situation was so tense, we saw men in black suits around our home day and night. Although my parents never said so, I knew they had lost several contacts. My mom freaked out. She urged my dad to destroy everything that could criminalize him, including these books. I knew how important they were to my dad, so one night I put them with bags of livestock feed in a pushcart and pushed them to a nearby pigsty. I covered them with rags and pig manure. It was so stinky that I believed no policemen would bother to search there."

When all the books had been put away, Abilene approached Phil and said in lowered voice, "We don't talk about my family's past at home, so please do not mention what we just talked about."

"I understand." But Phil didn't really understand. After all, it had been a long time, and Taiwan had become a different society now.

Phil, Abilene and her parents dined together

that night, although there were fewer dishes, Phil felt the food tasted even better than the New Year Eve feast from two years ago. After dinner, Abilene's parents vacated a room where Phil could crash. Before going to bed, he couldn't help but ask Abilene, "Don't they oppose your decision to give up the high paying job and move back here?"

Abilene smiled, "They don't know how much I make, and even if they did, they wouldn't care."

Abilene told Phil she was going to study sociology in college, but her parents warned her not to touch politics.

"Sociology is not politics."

"It could be very political, so I picked a business school instead. Anyway, Marx's *Capital* had been banned until the 90s. What would be the point of studying sociology without Marxism and The Frankfurt School?"

"It would be like Kong-Pao Chicken without chicken."

"Impossible to swallow." They laughed.

***

At home Daphne began to read news right after taking a shower. Updates of the strike on digital media poured in, and from non-mainstream media, she read analysis on the first large strike for decades in Taiwan together with issues of neo-liberalism, market rules, and free trade. The new proletariats in the post-industrial era included people from the service industries, and the battlefields of class conflict were in the streets of the cities, compared to the past when it happened in or around the factories. Exactly! She was convinced that she and her fellow flight attendants were 100% proletariats without any productive tools. She read on: "the digital devices might have changed the means of communication and the patterns of economies, but it never changed the nature of exploitation." Yes, well said. Free trade agreements between nations have become the most powerful method to serve multinational corporations, at the price of the benefits of farmers, laborers, and consumers. Thus resistance must process from different paths with differentiated strategies, from the side of production as well as from the side of consumption.

So their strike was actually connected to the occupation of parliament by students two years ago?! The free trade agreement between Taiwan and China was believed to be very harmful to farmers and small businesses, and only large corporations benefitted, for they could import cheaper materials, cheaper laborers and cheaper service. She never really figured out what might happen once the free trade agreement was signed, but out of her distrust of the government and the more and more brazen measures taken by large companies against allowing their employees to have more holidays and higher compensation for extra works, she had no doubt that the students must be right about the negative influence of the free trade.

Daphne knew she needed some sleep but she couldn't. She also knew it was impossible to sort out any answer for such a complex situation but she felt restless to absorb information about it. A lot more keywords needed to be explored.... At last she decided she was too tired to do any further research and should take off for their second round of gathering in front of the airline headquarters.

Back to the street, the temperature had dropped significantly, some of the old faces from last night returned, some new faces joined them.

***

The next morning, Phil was treated to a breakfast of rice porridge with yams in it, freshly fried fish and several dishes of preserved vegetables. Then Abilene drove him to the High Speed Railway station.

"One thing I have to ask you. When I made the mistake of confusing 'up limit' and 'lower limit,' you could have just turned me in and got rid of me, I know I am not particularly productive in your team, why did you cover up for me?"

"When a team is working on a task, it is like a runners' relay race. The one given the baton runs as fast as he can and as far as he is allowed until he no longer can make it. He gives the baton to anyone who is able to continue, and does not blame anyone who runs slower or not far enough. Everyone has different obstacles to overcome and dilemmas to face. We are not in any position to condemn anyone. That's the mentality I learned from my father, on account of what he fought for, along with all the nameless, faceless heroes and martyrs."

When Phil was deeply touched by what Abilene said, she added in a cold voice, "But do not have an illusion of comradeship, I defended you because you are, generally speaking, creating more value for our output than troubles. It's still the cruel rules of capitalism."

***

After five days in the streets, one night they were told that the CEO of their airline was replaced by the board, all of them applauded cheerfully. The union told the news media again that what they asked for—to reschedule the inhuman working hours—would never change, no matter who was the CEO.

Around midnight the union representatives

returned with good news: their harsh new working schedule was withdrawn. A schedule no worse than the one they had would be decided in three days and before that time any member of the union could decide whether they wanted to work or not. It was quick. They actually had prepared to be in the street for at least one week. Daphne knew as flight attendants they were lucky because their strike could attract great attention from the public, compared to other workers from textile factories or highway toll booths.

She went to fill in the flight schedule in the following three days, she knew that the earlier they started working the earlier the pissed off passengers would spare the ground staff. She wanted to fly to London, the admirable city she never had time to explore.

***

In the meeting at 7:45 a.m., one and a quarter hours before the trading of stock market began, Molly told everybody she has downgraded her view of the airline.

"You downgraded it when the strike began, and now the strike is over, you downgrade it again?" Phil asked.

"Yes, I've calculated, according the new deal between its administration with the flight attendants, it will eat up its profit up to around 13 million USD a year."

Phil sat back, thinking how absurd this world has become. When a corporation has more humane working conditions, it must be downgraded for its potential investors.

"Merry Christmas." As the meeting was dismissed, Phil said to his hard-working colleagues who seemed unaware and unimpressed that it was Christmas.

Legacy

There was a commotion among the protesters sitting ahead of Chung-Ming, who realized there must be some police action going on. In fact, that's exactly why they were here. All of them sat, one next to another as closely as possible, with their hands holding one another as tight as possible. They have been here for three hours, Chung-Ming started feeling hungry, and he knew the police also were well aware of it. They waited until all the protesters were exhausted before expelling them.

During the three hours water bottles had been passed on carefully, when one got it, he or she loosened one hand to take the bottle from the person next to him at one side, who had just loosened his or her other hand to take the bottle. So they could drink water and their hands had several seconds to relax in turn. When one has done with the water bottle, their hands held again. Then Chung-Ming felt his hand were massaged by the person passing on the water from his right side, so he started massaging the hand of the person he just passed the water on his left. The waves of taking care one another were passing on and on, Chung-Ming's heart was warmed.

Chung-Ming was actually glad the police were taking action, he wished it to be ended soon because he was so tired. He had a quarrel with his boyfriend last night, it was more energy consuming than anything. They had been together nearly four years, and recently his being unemployed became a problem between them because living expenses in Taipei went up so much. Chung-Ming wanted to be a novelist, he wanted to write about the dark side of cities, the helplessness and haplessness of people in cities. But it was not a practical plan for the future, what had been his idealism became a burden in his relationship.

Chung-Ming couldn't help but wondering, were the people next to him holding his hands so tightly homophobic? What would they respond if they knew he was gay?

The commotion in the front rows seemed to be elevated, some of them were moving. Screams of girls could be heard, followed by shouts of boys around them. Now Chung-Ming saw that they were not moving, they were split by police one by one and carried away. Obviously the actions of splitting their tightly held hands caused great pain, and some girls began to cry, and boys next to them tried to push away the police.

Now he saw they were circled by hundreds of policemen with shields and batons, Chung-Ming's heart skipped a beat. The circle was getting smaller and smaller as the policemen were approaching the protesters. Should he resist as much as he could? Or should he avoid getting himself hurt? But before he could make up his mind, the police had already got him and the people next to him. The boy on his right began to forcefully kick the two policemen pulling them apart, so Chung-Ming also began to struggle wildly, and the two policemen hit back with their batons mercilessly. It really hurt, Chung-Ming thought, nevertheless he fought even more furiously.

"Cuff them up!" A voice with authority ordered.

Then during the kicking and tearing Chung-Ming felt he was pulled up-side-down suddenly and when his vision was back again his head was relentlessly being smashed on the ground, and his hands were cuffed at his back before he was violently thrown into the back of a police van. He couldn't tell where the pain was from- his head, his shoulder or his hip.

In the police station he was seated with several other protesters, one of their hands was cuffed to an iron metal bar fixed to the wall. The police handled things slowly on purpose, they rang the prosecutor but hung up immediately, saying, "The D.A. is busy." Leaving their detainees sitting there uncomfortably thirsty and hungry.

Suddenly Chung-Ming felt a buzzing in the back pocket of his jeans, he realized the cell phone he had held temporarily for his teacher from graduate school had been with him since last night. They met up shortly before he left the protest and his teacher joined the protest for the night. Chung-Ming took out the cell phone and answered.

"Hello,"

An old woman's voice spoke in Taiwanese, "What's going on there?"

"This is not Professor Kao, this is Wang Chung-Ming, his student." Chung-Ming replied with his not so fluent Taiwanese.

"So where is your teacher now?"

"I don't know... I... I am in the police station...."

"You are arrested?"

"Yes. We were protesting...."

"Which police station?" The woman seemed to be aware of the situation, she did not wait until Chung-Ming finished his explanation.

"Da-An Station."

"I will send a lawyer over now. What's your name again?"

"Chung-Ming, Wang Chung-Ming."

"Good. Your lawyer will be there soon," then the phone was hung up.

A policeman stood up from his desk and walked toward him, trying to grab his cell phone, Chung-Ming resisted, "I have the right to make a phone call."

"You just made it."

"No, I answered a phone call, now I am making a phone call."

Chung-Ming dialed the number of his friend Buo-Kai.

"This is Chung-Ming."

"Where are you, bro?"

"In Da-An Police Precinct."

"Fuck!"

"Someone said a lawyer will be coming to represent me."

"Who is someone?"

"I don't know."

"I will check around and see what we can do, bro." Bou-Kai briefed him on the situation of the other protesters, most of them were all right except some had slight bruises. They were having meetings to talk about what steps to take next.

About half an hour later, a lawyer showed up. A young man who looked like he was going to a party instead of the court.

"What charge do you have for Mr. Wang Chung-Ming?" He inquired of the policemen on duty.

"Violation of the *Assembly and Parade Act*." A policeman answered.

"How long has it been since you did your homework? Don't you know the Supreme Court has ruled that the *Assembly and Parade Act* is against the Constitution Law? People are free to gather up in anywhere they like without needing to tell you in advance."

Another policeman quickly corrected, "Obstruction of Law Enforcement."

"What law you guys were enforcing?" The young lawyer asked with contempt, "Forcing people out of their homes, I see." He added to himself.

Chung-Ming was bailed out, together with all the other protesters. The cell phone was returned to him, and he called back to the old woman to thank her, although Chung-Ming wondered how he was going to pay for the lawyer's legal service.

"I am released, thanks."

"I am having dinner with your teacher at Jinhwa Noodle tonight, come to join us."

Jinhwa Noodle Store was near where he was arrested, only one lane away from the Sinolight Community. Before the community was scheduled for demolition, the noodle store was a humble stall by the side exit of the community. People in this neighborhood often got takeout there, and taxi drivers dined there in the night. The yellow light from the light bulbs hanging from the wall warmed people in the night, although the electricity came from some suspicious source. In the age before the convenient stores found everywhere, people working overnight or students studying late could get some noodles here for late night snack.

There were four people for the dinner, his teacher Prof. Kao and his mother who was the caller and his savior, and the lawyer who bailed him out. They had dried noodles with sticky and oily sesame paste, fish ball soup, greens, and beer. It was like a family gathering, they chatted about common things like every night after an uneventful day. Chung-Ming ate quietly, it was the first meal he had for a whole day. Prof. Kao seemed to notice how hungry Chung-Ming was, he ordered pig feet for him and told him it was for his release from the detention. It's a custom in Taiwan to have pig feet after bad things happened, so the bad luck won't come again.

After dinner they walked past the site of their protest, after the evacuation in the morning it was barricaded by barbed wire and spired steel barricades. Bulldozers would come any day to demolish the old houses. The lawyer took out a cigarette and lit it, his eyebrows burrowed when gazing at the evacuated buildings, then he breathed out a big whiff of cigarette smoke. The memories a city contains are worth nothing compared to the capital a development could generate through urban gentrification. Before departing, Chung-Ming learned from his business card that the lawyer's name was Wu Chih-Hsin. He still looked like he was going to a party.

Chung-Ming went home and took a shower to wash away all the dirt he got from sitting by the rubble for three hours and all afternoon in the police station. His boyfriend was away, but from the rearranged items of their room, Chung-Ming felt that they might make up soon. He really did not have more energy to fight, he crashed and fell asleep immediately.

Prof. Kao's mother was called Grandma Kao by the students of his son. She made delicious kimchi and many of them were given a jar every time she made a batch. The lawyer Wu Chih-Hsin's fee for representing Chung-Ming was two jars of kimchi. "Democratic Kimchi", the lawyer received them happily.

"Democratic Kimchi" had a long history dating back to the 1970s, when Grandma Kao was still a housewife in her thirties. One time her husband told her that he had a friend studying in Michigan wishing to set up a periodical but had no money, he felt obliged to find money for his friend.

"What kind of periodical he is establishing?"

"Social, political issues... a rather academic journal."

It was beyond Ms. Kao to perceive why a Taiwanese wanted to set up an academic journal about social and political issues in the US, and why her husband wanted to help him. Mr. Kao was working for a presbyterian church as a deacon, the pay was very thin and they could make their ends meet only because the church provided them with the monthly rent for a humble apartment, and their kids were able to take free programs organized by the church. It was really impossible to squeeze any extra money to assist his friend's dream. Mrs. Kao was worried, but she knew when her husband mentioned something, he must have made up his mind already.

The next morning Mrs. Kao suddenly found a way to make a little bit more money. When she came home from food market, she carried so many bags of napa cabbage, she hardly could stand straight.

"What are you doing?" Seeing his wife moving bags of vegetables awkwardly, Mr. Kao rushed to help her.

"I have a good idea to make some money to help your friend in the US."

Mr. Kao looked at the bags scattered all over the floor with a suspicious expression.

"I am making kimchi to sell."

"So you bought all these cabbage?"

"They are very cheap, that's why the idea of making kimchi occurred to me. The farmers have grown too much cabbage this year, so the prices fall to almost nothing. I got all these with just a couple of hundred bucks, and the vendors were so thankful."

"Good," Mrs. Kao was happy to hear that the solution served for all, "let me help, then. How to start?"

Mrs. Kao stood straight up, looking at her husband, bemused, "I don't know. I never made kimchi."

That was how the business of "Democratic Kimchi" began. In the age without internet, they had to ask around for the recipes of making kimchi and test out each way the were told. Kimchi was not traditional Taiwanese food, and information about Korean food or Japanese food was so partial or twisted. The first time they only made about 20 jars, most of the napa cabbage were wasted in failed attempts. But people helped them so much, some wrote letters to total strangers to ask for tips for them, some joined the labor, some just put money for future purchase, and some persuaded their neighbors to buy without knowing clearly why Mrs. Kao needed to make money from this business.

Later the "Democratic Kimchi" not only funded the journal, it also became the major source of the flight tickets for some political dissidents to sneak back to Taiwan. And after Mr. Kao was arrested and tortured for the alleged crime of treason, and finally killed in the prison, it was how Mrs. Kao sustained herself and raised up their three children.

Over the last two decades, when the post-martial-law society gradually opened up and the public awareness of the environmental conservation or cultural heritage preservation had been elevated, "Democratic Kimchi" helped activists raise money to organize their concerts or marches among other events. In some cases of more acute resistance against the law enforcement, "Democratic Kimchi" paid for the legal service. More and more lawyers joined the team of volunteer defenders, Wu Chih-Hsin was one of them.

Grandma Kao called Wu Chi-Hsin to represent Chung-Ming also because Wu Chih-Hsin was born and raised up in the Sinolight Community, where dormitories for judges and prosecutors were built and they had lived for decades. The compounds consisting three four-floor structures with an atrium in each structure provided children the safest places to play. Here they had played soccer, learned how to ride bicycles, and raced their wall climbing skills. Wu Chih-Hsin's father was the chief judge of a criminal appellate court, who lived in this community to the end of his life. Wu Chih-Hsin vaguely learned his father's ambivalent feelings towards this nation he had fought for during the World War. He knew his father had been under surveillance all the time, although he never talked about it.

When the city government announced its plan to develop this area in the model of Manhattan, judges and prosecutors were relocated, but quite a few poor families that had set up along the fringes had no place to go. They'd made the simply constructed shacks along the community their homes since moving to Taiwan from China. To evict them, the government sued them for illegally occupying public land, demanding not only their immediate evacuation but also monetary compensation that appeared to be astronomical numbers to them. Had they the money, why would they stay in the slum-like area? It was so absurd for Chung-Ming and his fellow activists to see the government deeming the right to property higher than the basic needs of people. Although from their earlier experience of protesting, like tree sitting or anti-nuclear demonstrations, they knew by no means could they stop the state violence, but their actions would bring public attention and debates, which helped engage people to look into the very questionable development. But that was why Chung-Ming's boyfriend felt so insecure. He was OK with Chung-Ming's social movements, but the unpredictable life style and unexpected expense resulted from Chung-Ming's increasingly radical resistance agonized him. Sometimes he blamed Prof. Kao for leading Chung-Ming to the risks that he couldn't afford. Prof. Kao might be admired and followed by many young people, but he should not suppose that everyone in his passionate cult was clear about what consequences might occur.

Prof. Kao studied urban planning in the US with scholarships his advisers found for him. After graduate school, he worked for an architecture firm in Pennsylvania for seven years. His mother once believe that her son might just settle down in the US, which suited his talents and rebellious ideas better. But he moved back to Taiwan and involved more and more in political activities. It appalled Grandma Kao. Their family was still on the Black List of the dissidents then, and the nightmares of her husband being tortured to death reemerged.

They said Mr. Kao was a traitor, a separatist, for the independence of Taiwan from the Republic of China. Compared to some cultures today, when a place wants to be independent from a nation, it could be debated openly or decided by referendum. Separatism in the past could have cost tens of thousands of lives was so unbelievable. On the other hand, Grandma Kao also was very clear that in the past the government would find any excuse to silence people who talked loudly about public affairs and criticized public policies. Their loyalty or patriotism to their nation was just an excuse to subdue them. Without oppressive measures, the legitimacy of the exiled government in Taiwan could be overturned by people who suffered the inequality between social classes, who condemned the corrupt officials, or people who never identified the regime as their ruler. In a society silenced for so long, many problems then were still problems now, only people were free to discuss them today. The coming and going of politicians were totally normal now, they were no longer worshipped like superheroes.

Prof. Kao resembled his father so much, although he hardly remembered him. Those dreadful days of being stalked, checked and harassed by law enforcement and secret service from time to time even after years of Mr. Kao's death were never gone afar enough. Nevertheless, Grandma Kao knew it was useless to stop her son. Fortunately, thanks to the fights of his father and his fellow dissidents decades ago, expressing different ideas today was much safer. Prof. Kao had been cuffed up and brought to the police station many times, but was never charged. The law enforcement knew better that the resistance might elevate once the young people's leader was charged. It also knew that picking up younger activists was a more efficient strategy to frighten and dissuade people who thought of supporting them by joining the protests.

Knowing her son's freedom was given at the price of his students' confinement, Grandma Kao worked hard to make more "Democratic Kimchi" to thank them. Besides, after years of wrestling with the laws, Grandma Kao was very familiar with what legal measures they could take to protect their rights. Those dreadful memories of state violation of human rights were never far away.

Half an year later, Chung-Ming was sentenced to three months in jail, for obstruction of justice. Although he could choose to pay fine, he did not have the money to buy his freedom, and he also determined to do his time to emphasize that what he had obstructed was injustice, not justice. His lawyer appealed, with argument that protesting belonged to people's freedom of speech against state violence, so did their resistance to being arrested. He contended that the freedom of speech of this country was not comprehensive, for the government first used the *Assembly and Parade Act* to control people's activities, and after it was decided unconstitutional by the Supreme Court, the excuse of "Obstruction of Justice" was used in the most abusive manner.

To their disappointment, the appellate court dismissed their appeal, the decision of the district court was maintained. The good thing was, the development to duplicate a Manhattan in Taipei was put off.

Before going to jail, Chung-Ming, Prof. Kao, his lawyer and other protesters organized a press conference to loudly criticize the government's violation of human rights by forcing people from their homes first, then confining people expressing their disagreement. The dreadful violation of human rights by the state was never far away.

Chung-Ming brought two jars of "Democracy Kimchi" for his time in the prison. And when he began his days in the prison, he immediately realized that, the human rights of prisoners was another ugly issue needing to be dealt with.

Others' Guilt

Sitting at the writing table while his wife was preparing dinner, Chi-Jon noticed dust rising along the pathway that faced their kitchen window. Several minutes later a figure emerged, running toward their house.

It was Little Lu, one of Chi-Jon's former students. Little Lu ran all the way to their doorstep. Seeing him rushing, Chi-Jon got to his feet quickly to open their back door. The boy stopped to catch his breath, while stammering, "Mr. Sun, Mr. Hsu is in trouble!"

"Hsu Ching-Hsiung?"

"Yes. They found his… his certificate of the… communist member?" The boy seemed not quite sure what he was saying, as though he were passing on messages understood only by adults.

"Hsu Ching-Hsiung is a communist?" Chi-Jon asked but immediately understood that it was useless to raise the question to this boy standing in front of him with an expression of total unknowing. Chi-Jon had been aware that Hsu Ching-Hsiung was participating in various politically active groups with sometimes radical opinions, but he'd never imagined that Hsu Ching-Hsiung would become a communist.

"They picked him up?"

"No. He was away when the police came to his home, and then he ran away when he heard about the search."

"So where is he now?"

The boy pointed toward the woods behind him. Chi-Jon started in the direction of the woods but was stopped by his wife Su-Jen, "No, don't go, you'll disclose his hiding place if you go." She turned to Little Lu, "You go, but come back here two hours later, when the sky is completely darkened. When you come back, you can tell us what Mr. Hsu needs. Go back to town now, but walk, don't run. Pretend you just visited us to borrow a book from your teacher. Be calm, understand me?"

The boy nodded. Su-Jen went into the house and grabbed several buns and a jacket. "The jacket is for Mr. Hsu, and the buns you can share with him." Before Little Lu took off, Su Jen put her hands on his shoulders, comforting him, "Don't be afraid; we are doing the right thing. We just cannot let others know at this moment, OK?"

Little Lu walked away, calmer. Chi-Jon was surprised that his wife was handling the whole incident so strategically. She reminded him of a character from a detective novel.

"Police are all the same," she said. Whether Japanese police or Chinese police, they are not protecting us from villains; they are the villains. Some of my ancestors and their friends were persecuted by the police and their bosses in the government. It was ugly."

She made extra food that night: chicken, steamed rice, boiled eggs and cucumber. She wrapped the food with a towel to keep it warm, and put it in a worn-out bag people would usually use for grocery shopping. When all the preparation was done, Little Lu appeared. Su Jen gave him a chunk of chicken to eat, and instructed him, "This towel wrapping the food is for Mr. Hsu to clean himself. I believe he will be able to find some river water near him. He also can use the towel as a filter for drinking water."

After eating the delicious dinner Su-Jen had provided, Little Lu left with the bag. He was a member of the Tsou Tribe, extremely good hikers, even during the difficult seasons.

"Luckily it's May now; otherwise Hsu Ching-Hsiung would have a problem surviving in the woods," Chi-Jon said. He had suggested bringing more things for him, but Su Jen told him that the less stuff he carried, the easier it would be for him to hide, or run, if necessary.

A communist. Chi-Jon did not really understand what it meant. Hsu Ching-Hsiung was a judicial scrivener. He earned his educational degree and professional certificate in Shanghai. When the Nationalist government took over Taiwan from Japan, Hsu Ching-Hsiung joined the governmental teams for the so-called Land Reform and traveled all over the island. But he returned after about two or three years and worked as a paralegal in the town down the hill. When asked why he had given up the promising career, Hsu just ambiguously said that he couldn't fit into that kind of working culture. "They are people with high status and high taste, you know. I came from a humble upbringing, and I feel more comfortable with the lifestyle of the working class."

They overheard that officials who had come from the Chinese Nationalist government tended to use public funds for their personal activities, such as drinking and partying. And when they traveled, they demanded that local businesses treat them to free accommodations, and even offer them gifts. They believed that they were bringing prosperity to impoverished villages and people should feel thankful. Hsu felt excluded by his colleagues, for he did not know what good wine, good food, or a good outfit was. He did not know the cities in China they were talking about and couldn't comprehend the jokes they told. Was that the reason why Hsu Ching-Hsiung had become a communist, the enemy of the nationalists? Chi-Jon knew that Hsu Ching-Hsiung was an opportunist to a certain degree, but what had brought him to become a member of an extremely controversial political party was a mystery. He couldn't be so naive to believe that being the enemy of the ruling party would give him any advantage, could he?

The following days they had Little Lu bringing food to Hsu Ching-Hsiung in the wood between the town and the hamlet where Chi-Jon and his wife lived. They pretended that the boy was coming to take sketching classes from his former art teacher, for he planned to study art in Taipei. They also fabricated several sketches in order to disguise his visits. But the situation turned dire, they were told that the searches and arrests were becoming nationwide actions, and more troops arrived in Keelong Harbor from China to put down the uprising throughout the islands. Chi-Jon and Su-Jen were worried that Hsu Ching-Hsiung would be found by either the local police or the soldiers sent from China.

"We will have to give him a new identity."

Su-Jen said.

"What do you mean a new identity?"

"Make new identity papers for him."

So Su-Jen looked into their old documents, certificates and papers, and told Chi-Jon to produce something with a similar appearance to those examples. "No one really knows what a government document should look like, but if we make a paper showing that Mr. Hsu has an assignment of a government position, he will be able to get away. Mr. Hsu speaks perfect Mandarin, so no one would suspect he is not a Chinese mainlander.

They tore a paper from an art catalogue that was about five years old with a color comparable to the documents they had found at home. Then Chi-Jon started making stamps out of rubber erasers. An assignment of a governmental position must consist of three stamps: a big red stamp of the Republic of China, a small red stamp of the authority assigning the job, and a blue stamp representing Chiang Kai-Shek. It took at least seven or eight erasers to make them, so they had to ask Little Lu to buy them from town. Fortunately as an art pupil, Little Lu had a good reason to buy a lot of rubber erasers.

Chi-Jon and Su-Jen assigned Hsu Ching-Hsiung to the position of an interpreter of the Garrison Command. It was a vague position that purportedly involved monitoring and wiring people among other tasks of surveillance. They figured that very few people knew whether this position really existed or not, even people in the high ranks of the government. Since the entire society was under such chaos, it would be unlikely that the authenticity of the documents would be checked.

After the stamps were carefully pressed upon the paper, Chi-Jon folded it several times and left it in a humid environment, and then exposed it to sunlight. He hoped to create a feeling that it had been carried in person secretly for years. They carefully put the paper in an envelope for Little Lu to bring to the wood. Chi-Jon and Su-Jen did not explain what it was to Little Lu, thinking he was too young to understand it.

***

The news that Little Lu had killed his employer in Taipei was a crushing blow to Chi-Jon and Su-Jen. They had assumed that Little Lu was an artist in the city, and of course that meant that he would have taken odd jobs because an artist can hardly support himself on his art alone. That was why they felt so devastated when they learned the truth: since Little Lu had left for Taipei, he had never had a chance to learn art because he worked sixteen hours a day in the dry cleaning business, without a life of his own. Being a young man without much formal education, he couldn't communicate clearly in Chinese, and he had been reprimanded continuously by his employer who had taken away his I.D. Card. Little Lu found no help, no hope and no escape. The deprivation of his independence and dignity eventually drove him to murder.

Chi-Jon couldn't sleep for days. The beautiful face of Little Lu from many years ago emerged constantly in his dreams. He had been a restless boy in his class, never able to concentrate for more than ten minutes, but Chi-Jon knew that you couldn't imprison a mountain youth in the classroom. He should be hunting ferocious beasts in the forest, wading across dangerous waters, or shouting brave war songs into the gorges. He did not belong in the classroom, watercoloring the small shrubs that grew beside the campus running tracks.

Imagining how horrible it could be for Little Lu to be confined in the small room of the laundry shop made Chi-Jon's heart break. Had he known! Had he known! He cried in his sleep and when he was awake. He wished he had never stopped his contact with Little Lu after he went to Taipei. He was so naive to be convinced that Little Lu would have succeeded in his pursuit of an art career in such a hostile city. Tribal people could barely survive in cities where they struggled so desperately with the discrimination and repression that society imposed on them.

The court sentenced Little Lu to death according to the criminal law that commanded "Whosoever commits murder shall suffer death". The trial was moved to the appellate court, and Little Lu's attorney pleaded that the criminal law ordaining the death penalty to murderers without considering the causes of their killing was unconstitutional. So the appellate court ordered an investigation into Little Lu's psychological condition. Unfortunately, the investigation resulted in a decision that Little Lu was sound enough to bear responsibility for his brutal behavior, so the death sentence stood.

People from all the tribes initiated a special petition for Little Lu's amnesty. It was the first time such an action had been taken by all the tribes in Taiwan. They told the public that blaming Little Lu only showed how unjust the society was toward indigenous peoples. The discrimination and exploitation of tribal people had a long history and had never been indemnified. The petition won great sympathy from the public as well as some law experts. They tried every possible means to save Little Lu, even extraordinary appeal. But extraordinary appeal was designed for procedural mistakes found in decided cases. The appeal had to be filed by the Supreme Prosecutors Office, though it seemed unlikely to happen because that office kept playing the petition down. But Su-Jen reminded Chi-Jon that Hsu Ching-Hsiung was the Deputy Prosecutor General.

Over the decades Chi-Jon and Su-Jen had no doubt that Hsu Ching-Hsiung not only escaped the disaster of being found a communist, but also climbed up the bureaucratic ladder by making good use of the fake certificate they had manufactured for him. They recognized the irony at the same time that they felt a sense of pride in the techniques they had used to fake the document, "These officials must have been idiots to believe him and his proof." As a communist converted into a nationalist, this villain in the eye of the ruling class had made himself a dignitary among them.

Chi-Jon decided to write Hsu Ching-Hsiung a letter:

Respected Sir:
I write this letter on behalf of our mutual friend Lu Tam-Sheng, who is sentenced to capital punishment for his mistake. It is an unforgivable crime he has committed, but as a badly tormented young man with very limited

perspective and social support, he did not see any opportunity to break through his plight.

I am humbly urging you, our greatly respected Deputy Prosecutor General, to look into his suffering. Once you understand what he has gone through, you would never hesitate to file an extraordinary appeal for Tam-Sheng. You must remember, back in the year of the turmoil in our hometown, what a compassionate boy he was. He risked his own life to help our townsmen survive during that most dangerous time by bringing indispensable materials to everyone in need.

Please forgive my rudeness for writing this letter, but Little Lu's life is at stake, and I can't think of any other way to address the injustice that the people of my community are facing. I am convinced that the last legal action, the extraordinary appeal, eventually will bring justice, which is the only hope for Little Lu and his tribesmen.

Yours faithfully,
Sun Chi-Jon

Chi-Jon was very clear that his letter was more a blackmail than it was a petition. By reminding Hsu Ching-Hsiung that Chi-Jon and his wife had produced the paper for his escape nearly twenty years ago, he hoped that Hsu Ching-Hsiung might feel a little threatened and do something for Little Lu.

A week later, Chi-Jon got a response from the office of the Deputy Prosecutor General:

To Mr. Sun:
Regarding your letter on 18/April, the office of Deputy Prosecutor General responds as follows:—
The Deputy Prosecutor General has never had any personal acquaintance with Mr. Lu Tam-Sheng, and thus had no any interaction with Mr. Lu before the trial or after the trial.
Court decisions are based on the legal professionalism of the judges, and the decision as to whether or not an extraordinary appeal should be filed is in the hands of juristic professionalism as well.

Regards
Office of Deputy Prosecutor General

Reading the letter, Chi-Jon and Su-Jen were extremely disappointed.

"He is not afraid that we might disclose his fake certificate?" Chi-Jon asked in despair.

"Who'd believe us? We had never thought of leaving some clues on the paper so that one day we might make use of them."

"Because our goal was to save him from being persecuted, not to help him make his way up in the bureaucracy."

The extraordinary appeal never was filed, and the amnesty did not happen. Little Lu was executed one and a half years later.

The day after Lu was executed, Chi-Jon walked to the village after leaving work, and went to look for Little Lu's home. An old man sitting in front of the shack was playing a small bamboo flute. It sounded like weeping. Chi-Jon gathered that the old man was playing an elegy for Little Lu, because he was a sinner and could not be buried by traditional rituals. Chi-Jon sat down by the old man quietly until he forgot how long he had been sitting there.

Little Lu's trial became a wake-up call for indigenous peoples in Taiwan. They established the Alliance of Taiwanese Indigenous Tribes to work on the rights of their people. It kicked off political movements of these forgotten populations, and thoroughly changed the public's understanding of indigenous cultures in Taiwan.

***

Several years after the enactment of the *Freedom of Government Information Law*, tons of materials related to past political persecution were excavated. People were talking about transitional justice, insisting that perpetrators must be ferreted out, and criminal responsibility must be pursued. It had been a long fight. First the post-war massacre when the Nationalist Army took over Taiwan. Then the decades silenced by oppressive censorship and highly controlled public opinions. The secret arrests and confinement without due process of trial continued relentlessly. It didn't stop until the abolishment of Martial Law and the termination of the unjustified agencies that conducted these horrifying offenses.

One day Chi-Jon, now a retired old man, reads the newspaper with a headline:

Former Grand Justice Hsu Ching-Hsiung Found Involved in Human Rights Violation

The article explains that several units of the Garrison Command have been found to have seriously violated human rights since the late 40s by making unlawful arrests, torturing suspects; and encouraging vigilantism by the acquiescence of their authority. The illegal operations lasted into the late 80s, and among the piles of documents, a copy of Hsu Ching-Hsiung's job assignment as an interpreter of the Garrison Command has been dug out. Although the linkage of Hsu's wrongdoing during his time in the Garrison Command, had he really worked there, is circumstantial, the newspaper goes on to talk about the great shame of a former human rights oppressor becoming a grand justice. Some people interviewed by the reporters have demanded that his salary as a grand justice and his pension should be returned, and his entire career in the government should be investigated. Furthermore, all the legal opinions he had written for the supreme court during his seven years of service should be closely reviewed.

Former grand justice Hsu Ching-Hsiung, now in his eighties and retired, hasn't made any response yet, according to reports.

From the black-and-white picture on the newspaper, Chi-Jon still can see the faded prints of the stamps he manufactured more than fifty years ago. Time has made the document even more real.

Chi-Jon is stunned. He does not know whether he should speak up or not. But he remembers many many years ago when they were talking about the possibility of disclosing the fact that the document was actually produced by him and his wife, his late wife had said, "Who would believe us?"

A Letter From Father

Dear Kaiting:

The book *A Room With A View* that you and your mother selected for me finally arrived. I suppose the administration was checking it and could not find anything that violated the rules governing what we read here. You said you were impressed by the story that was featured in the film with the same name. The love story is indeed touching, and I think the film lightened the dark side of the story in order not to hurt the feelings of its caring audience members, like you. In the book, however, I see more about the inequality between different social classes.

In our place we do have windows with views, although I share a room with another thirty-one men. The windows at the head of our bunkbeds provide us light and air. Mine overlooks a corner of the sea, and between our building and the sea is a hill covered with wild plants and grass. It's about a half mile from my place to the hill, and probably another quarter mile from the hill to the sea. In certain weather we can hear the tides. It sounds like they are being rushed toward the shore by strong winds, but they resist staying there. When the movement caused by their battles turns violent, we hear the roaring winds and shouting waves. They never get tired of battling.

The trees over the hill never fail to catch my eyes. How can they thrive in the gusty winds and the salty air? Some of the trees look like their trunks have been burned, but their leaves still stretch energetically in every direction. From here, I detect that in certain seasons there will be orange fruits growing under the strong branches; they have the shape of pineapples, but pineapples grow on the ground, not on trees. There are also trees similar to the bishop wood in our yard, but my judgement from this distance is probably not very accurate, because I am not sure bishop wood can survive in such a rough environment. Next to these trees there is pampas grass and something that looks like dog's-tail grass. They seem to be fighting for sunlight, but invariably the trees with solid trunks that can reach to the sky win over. Of course this is all from my imagination; I never really know what is going on there.

In the night when I can't sleep, I will look out into the pitch darkness and imagine these trees actually walking away without being noticed and then coming back before dawn to where they had been. One day they might just leave the hill for good, because who would care?

I wonder what else is on the hill. If I checked from the windows at the head of my roommates' bunkbeds I might see something else, but in this overcrowded place everybody maintains a distance from one another. We don't know the personal history of the others. I think the first thing I do when I get out of here, I'll walk to the hill to check out the trees. Are they growing upon fertile soil or upon rocky earth?

Dear daughter, you are like a tree that I planted fifteen years ago, and the only thing I expect of you is to stand straight. I know that with a father in prison, it can't be easy. I've failed to provide you with a life of triumphs. There is no clear road in my life leading me to a certain destination or the achievement of specific goals. I only know that I chose the road my conscious told me to take, and looking back, I don't regret it. I am paying a much higher price than I should have to pay, but I do not have remorse for I know of no other way around it. Although it is unfair and harsh, I've gotten support and love, and learned how to set my mind free when my body is confined. I have your mother and you growing stronger and tougher day by day from the soil in my chest. That will be more than I need to walk along this long, winding and desolate road.

I am worried that you won't be able to stand straight, my dearest daughter tree. I am worried that my situation might empty your heart, that you might lose your strength to stand firm. I want you to remember that your father might dissent against the authorities, but he is not a traitor to the country.

Kaiting, My dearest wish is that each letter I write you will bring you some of the nourishment you need. The long separation has inevitably brought me a great deal of anxiety and a sense of guilt. My thoughts of you and your mother stir in my mind day and night, but they also give me hope. I hope my words will become nutrition for your roots to absorb. I hope they help strengthen your will and your life's expectations. Being here gives me a bad name, but I hope my efforts will not be wasted in the gravel of despair, where trees have no chance to grow. I have been wronged, but I definitely don't want you to feel the same way throughout your precious time of youth.

At this moment I lift my head from the writing pad that sits on my knees, and I see through the window that the tall trees on the hill are reflecting sunlight while fluttering in the breeze. They are like millions of sequins, and are so carefree!

There is so much I want to say to you, but I will stop here now and wait for the writing of my next letter.

Love and peace,
Dad
March/28/1982

About the Author

C. J. Anderson-Wu(吳介禎)is a Taiwanese writer and literary activist known for her poignant works on Taiwan's history, particularly the period of military dictatorship known as the White Terror (1949-1987). In addition to her two collections of fiction, *Impossible to Swallow* (2017) and *The Surveillance* (2021), she is working on her third book, *Endangered Youth— To Hong Kong*.

Her works have been recognized internationally and have been shortlisted for numerous literary awards, including the Art of Unity Creative Award by the International Human Rights Art Festival and the Flying Island Poetry Manuscript Competition. She has also won the Strands Lit International Flash Fiction Competition, the Invisible City Blurred Genre Literature Competition, and the Wordweavers Literature Contest.

Author	C. J. Anderson-Wu
Publisher	Kanda Yasuko Momorial Foundation
Editors	Ginny Jaramillo, Steven M. Anderson
Art Editor	Ya-Yun Chung
Cover Photo	Poly Chen
ISBN	978-986-94977-0-1
Date	July 2017
Cover Price	10 USD, 300 NTD

www.ingramcontent.com/pod-product-compliance
Lightning Source LLC
LaVergne TN
LVHW021822060526
838201LV00058B/3477